STUDIES IN GENESIS

STUDIES
IN GENESIS

By

GEORGE HENDERSON

(Author of "The Pearl of Psalms")
"Studies in Hebrews" etc.

Published by

B. McCall Barbour
28 GEORGE IV BRIDGE, EDINBURGH 1
SCOTLAND

MADE AND PRINTED IN GREAT BRITAIN BY
STANLEY L. HUNT (PRINTERS) LTD., GEORGE STREET, RUSHDEN, NORTHANTS

CONTENTS

CHAPTER ONE

INTRODUCTION TO THE BOOK

THE book of Genesis has been called "the stately portal to the magnificent edifice of Scripture"; and that saying admirably describes the place which it holds in the sacred canon. It leads the reverent worshipper into the presence, and unveils the power and divinity, of the eternal God. The great fundamental questions of the human mind—Who? When? How? Why?—are answered here; not exhaustively, but in sufficient degree to give reason a foothold, and the heart a resting place. We approach the study of it with reverence and humility, recognising that here for the first time God breaks the silence of eternity.

1. THE TITLE OF THE BOOK

The word "Genesis" was the technical term used by the philosophers of Alexandria to describe the origin of things; and it was given to this book by the scholars who, in 280 B.C., translated the Old Testament into Greek, in order to describe its subject matter. The Hebrew title of the book, however, is taken from its first word which means "In the beginning"; and this is really the key which unlocks the treasures of this portion of the sacred volume. Here, among other things, we find the beginning of:

1.	The Universe	Genesis 1. 1.
2.	The Human Race	Genesis 1. 27.
3.	The Sabbath	Genesis 2. 1-3.
4.	Marriage	Genesis 2. 24.
5.	Sin	Genesis 3. 6.
6.	Prophecy	Genesis 3. 15.
7.	The Family	Genesis 4. 1-2.
8.	Sacrifice	Genesis 4. 4.

9.	Death	Genesis 4. 8.
10.	Human Government	Genesis 9. 1-6.
11.	Nations	Genesis 11.
12.	The Hebrew Race	Genesis 12. 1-2.

The subsequent history and development of these things are found in the later books of Scripture, and their ultimate end in the book of Revelation.

2. AUTHORSHIP AND AUTHENTICITY

Genesis was written about 1500 B.C., and the uniform testimony of Hebrew and Christian tradition ascribes its authorship to Moses, the law-giver of Israel. Each of the eight New Testament writers either quotes from it or refers to it; so also does the Lord Jesus Christ Himself. The following quotations from the New Testament writings cover the fifty chapters of Genesis.

1. "For in those days shall be affliction, such as was not from the beginning of the creation which God created unto this time." (Mark 13. 19).
   The reference is to Genesis 1. 1.

2. "Have ye not read that He which made them at the beginning made them male and female and said: 'for this cause shall a man leave father and mother, and shall cleave to his wife; and they twain shall be one flesh'?". Matthew 19. 3-5
   The reference is to Genesis 1. 26-27 and 2. 24.

3. "Adam was not deceived, but the woman being deceived was in the transgression." (1 Timothy 2. 14).
   The reference is to Genesis 3.

4. "For this is the message that we heard from the beginning, that we should love one another. Not as Cain who was of that wicked one and slew his brother." (1 John 3. 11-12).
   The reference is to Genesis 4.

5. "By faith Enoch was translated that he should not see death." (Hebrews 11. 5).
   The reference is to Genesis 5.

6. "God spared not the angels that sinned . . . and spared not the old world, but saved Noah, the eighth person, . . . bringing in the flood upon the world of the ungodly." (2 Peter 2. 4-5).
   The reference is to Genesis chapters 6 to 10.

7. Stephen's speech, Acts 7. 2-16, and Hebrews 11. 8-22, cover the remaining portion of the book of Genesis chapters 11 to 50.

I have quoted these passages at length in order to show you that the writers of the New Testament take for granted the historicity and truthfulness of the narratives of Genesis, and find in them some of the great foundation facts upon which they rear the structure of Christian doctrine. Indeed a recent writer speaks the sober truth when he says that "Genesis is the seed-plot of the Bible; it is essential to the true understanding of its every part; it is the foundation on which rests the whole of the revelation from God to man, and on which such revelation is built up. It is not only the foundation of all truth, but it also enters into, and forms part of, all subsequent Inspiration."

The question now arises: whence did Moses get this account of the origin of things? Not from any human source evidently; for man was not in existence to witness some of the scenes described. Not from the light of nature or of reason; for while nature proclaims, and reason perceives God's boundless power and matchless skill by the things which are made, neither of them can tell *how* these things were made. There is but one alternative: Moses received it by revelation from God, and wrote it by inspiration of God. (2 Peter 1. 21; Hebrews 11. 3).

It would be well for the people of God to recognise once for all that the men of science who, by their guesses are seeking to discredit the statements of the book of Genesis, are no more entitled to do so than the untutored savage at his kraal. "A man of science is no more fitted to theorise about the first cause and final end of the universe than the humblest man who looks on the world with a plain understanding and a simple heart. God and the soul are no nearer to a microscope or a telescope than to the eye." Science has to do with phenomena; it is the reasoned account of ascertained facts; but the beginning and the end of things are hidden from it. Where science must confess its ignorance and impotence Genesis steps in, and with the authority of God describes things which are otherwise unknowable. Science is confined to the realm of discoverable knowledge; Revelation is knowledge imparted by the Creator Himself.

3. HISTORICAL SCOPE

Genesis covers about 2,500 years of human history—from the creation of Adam to the death of Joseph. It is the oldest trustworthy record in the world, and contains information which cannot be found anywhere else. The main time divisions are as follows:

From Adam to the Flood—1656 years.

From the Flood to the call of Abram—427 years.

From the call of Abram to the death of Joseph—400 years.

Observe that Abram stands midway between Adam and Christ, and is thus the central figure of the Old Testament.

4. DIVISIONS

Genesis has been divided in various ways by different expositors. Some have divided it by the subjects with which it deals, others by the events which it records, and others again by the great names which it contains.

(A)   Dr. Morgan, for example, divides thus:

    (a) Generation—Chapters 1 and 2.

    (b) Degeneration—Chapters 3 to 11.

    (c) Regeneration—Chapters 12 to 50.

(B)   Dr. Patterson speaks of it as giving the history of three families:

    (a) The family of Adam—Chapters 1 to 5.

    (b) The family of Noah—Chapters 6 to 11.

    (c) The family of Abram—Chapters 12 to 50.

In these we see God's plan for man physically, socially, and spiritually.

(C) The natural divisions of the book, such as would appeal more particularly to a Hebrew student of the Scriptures, are as follows:

  (a) The introduction—chapter 1. 1. to 2. 3.
  (b) The eleven generations—chapter 2. 4. to 50. 26. The word "generations" here refers to the phrase, "these are the generations" which occurs eleven times in the fifty chapters.

(D) But for us who are readers of the English Bible with its chapters and verses, the division which I consider gives the clearest view of the book and the most practical help in mastering its contents is as follows:

	Primeval			Patriarchal	
	Chapters 1 to 11			Chapters 12 to 50	
(a)	Creation	1-2	(a)	Abraham	12-25
(b)	Fall	3-6	(b)	Isaac	21-28
(c)	Flood	7-9	(c)	Jacob	27-37
(d)	Nations	10-11	(d)	Joseph	37-50

Memorise these ten words; and if your reading of Genesis has been careful, you will be able by means of them to think your way through its contents.

To get an intelligent grasp of Genesis as a whole read it through at one sitting, and do this as frequently as possible. Do not stay to examine difficulties for the present; you can do that later. Do not go into details for the moment; you can use the microscope after you have made good use of the telescope. The book can be read through at an average pace in three hours.

CHAPTER TWO

THE FIRST CHAPTER OF GENESIS

IN this chapter we have brought before us in clear broad outline the facts of the beginning of the material universe, and of the preparation of the earth for man. Details such as can be furnished by the hammer of the geologist, the microscope of the scientist and the telescope of the astronomer are omitted; for, as someone has said, the Scriptures are written to tell us, not how the heavens go, but how we may go to Heaven. Bear well in mind, however, that while the outlook of Genesis is spiritual rather than scientific, it never has been found, it never will be found to be scientifically inaccurate. I make that statement on the authority of the greatest masters of geological, biological, and astronomical science. Sir J. W. Dawson, admittedly one of the ablest scientists of modern times, says that in his judgment "the first chapter of Genesis in the way in which it has anticipated discovery is itself a remarkable proof of the inspiration of the Bible. Those who attack Genesis either do not understand it or wilfully misrepresent it." He goes on to say that "those who base their hopes for the future on the revelations of the Bible, need not be ashamed of its story of the past." While our faith does not stand in the wisdom of men, it is interesting to find one who received the highest honours which the British Association for the advancement of Science can bestow, testifying thus to the scientific accuracy of this much-disputed portion of God's Word.

OUTLINE OF THE CHAPTER

1. Creation—Verse 1.
2. Destruction—Verse 2.
3. Reconstruction—Verses 3-31.

1. *Creation.* "In the beginning God created the heaven and the earth." Verse 1.

That is the most sublime and comprehensive sentence in human language. Although the very essence of simplicity, it stands unequalled in profound significance. It brings before us the living God—a personal, self existent Spirit—the first Source and Cause of all things; and by so doing sets aside at one stroke the seven great fundamental heresies which have misled the minds of men.

(a) Atheism affirms that there is no God: this verse reveals that there is.

(b) Deism declares that God cannot reveal Himself: the universe of Genesis 1. 1 is a revelation of His eternal power and Godhead (Romans 1. 20).

(c) Agnosticism says there may, or may not, be a God: but as design implies a designer, so creation implies a Creator.

(d) Materialism proclaims the eternity of matter: our verse says that in the beginning God created it.

(e) Pantheism says there is no God but the universe: we read here that the universe was summoned into existence by His command (Psalm 33. 9).

(f) Polytheism affirms that creation is the work of many gods: but that is disproved by the unity of nature: the same sun shines everywhere: the same laws of gravitation hold everywhere.

(g) Rationalism refuses to believe anything that transcends reason: but as man was not in existence at the time to which Genesis 1. 1 refers, the statement must be received by faith. It is through faith we understand, and faith, while ever unreasoning, is never unreasonable (Hebrews 11. 3).

Coming now to the words themselves, we find that they answer three questions: (1) What was created? The answer is "the heaven and the earth". (2) Who created them? The answer is "God". (3) When were they created? The answer is "In the beginning".

Regarding the answer to the last of these questions it should be noted that the phrase "in the beginning" speaks of "time without a date and space without a limit". That phrase is indicative of an indefinite and boundless past, the antiquity of which is beyond the computations of man. The supreme mistake which some chronologists have made—a mistake which is responsible for the disrepute into which, in many scientific minds, the first chapter of Genesis has fallen—is in reckoning their chronologies from the creation of the world. But carefully note that the first date recorded in the Word of God is in Genesis 5. 3; and that the point of time from which it is reckoned is the creation of man—not the creation of the world. Geologists tell us that the various strata of the earth must have taken millions of years to form, and this verse does not contradict that statement. It simply affirms that at a period in the dateless past which it calls "in the beginning," God created the heaven and the earth.

2.   *Destruction*. "And the earth was without form, and void; and darkness was upon the face of the deep." Verse 2.

The first thing which I want you to notice here is that the fourth word in this verse—the word "was"—is the same Hebrew word as in Genesis 19. 26 is translated "became"—('she became a pillar of salt'). And so verse 2 should read "the earth became waste and void." That God did not create it so, Scripture emphatically affirms. "Thus saith the Lord that created the heavens: God Himself that formed the earth and made it, He hath established it, He created it not in vain" (Isaiah 45. 18). The word which in Isaiah 45. 18 is translated "in vain" is the same word as in Genesis 1. 2 is translated "without form." God did not create it so; for some reason and at some subsequent time which have not been fully revealed to us, it became so. Eminent Bible students believe that somewhere between verses 1 and 2 there came into the perfect order of God's creation a catastrophe which changed cosmos into chaos, and perfect order into utter desolation. To this period of chaos belong the geological strata of the earth, and mark this significant fact: man is never found in a fossil state.

3. *Reconstruction.* Verses 3-31.

We have seen that at a certain period in remote antiquity called "in the beginning" God created the heaven and earth; that for some reason not fully disclosed but which certain hints in Scripture seem to connect with the fall of Satan, God's perfect order fell into utter confusion; and now from verse 3 onwards we behold our gracious God transforming chaos into cosmos, and preparing the earth for the new tenant—man.

"The earth was without form and void"—that is to say, it was formless, and it was empty. When we come to examine the work of the six reconstructive days we shall find that these two words "formless" and "empty" are the key to the literary structure of the chapter. The record of the first three days refers to the earth receiving its form, that of the last three days, to the filling up of its emptiness. As a matter of fact these are twin triads. In the second triad the work of the corresponding stage of the first triad is taken up and carried on to completion. Thus:

	Formless		Empty
Day 1.	Light.	Day 4.	Lights.
Day 2.	Firmament.	Day 5.	Fish; Fowl.
Day 3.	Dry Land.	Day 6.	Animals; Man.

Briefly, the work of the six days is as follows:

1st Day: Light (verses 3-5). "The existence of light before the appointment of the sun, and the arrangement of the solar functions which occurred on the fourth day, was long a puzzle to science. But science has recently discovered that there are more kinds of light than solar light and that it was perfectly in accordance with the facts of nature now fully known, that there should be light even before the sun became a luminous bearer of light for the solar system."

2nd Day: Formation of the firmament, or atmosphere, without which nothing in the animal or vegetable kingdom could live (verses 6-8).

3rd Day: Dry land and vegetation (verses 9-13). "Let the dry land appear." For a beautiful description of this work see Psalm 104. 5-9. Observe that in verse 11 you have the three great divisions of the vegetable kingdom—grasses, plants, and trees.

4th Day: Sun and Moon (verses 14-19). These, like the other parts of the universe, were created "in the beginning," but are here appointed to serve our earth as means of light and measures of time. The sun measures our days and years: the moon, our weeks and months.

5th Day: Creation of fish and birds (verses 20-23). Aerial life to inhabit the circumambient air: aquatic life to inhabit the liquid deep.

6th Day: Creation of land animals; creation of man (verses 24-31).

In the later books of the Old Testament God constantly appeals to His work in nature as the witness of His power, the evidence of His faithfulness, and the ground of His people's confidence.

"Who hath measured the waters in the hollow of His hand, and meted out heaven with the span, and comprehended the dust of the earth in a measure, and weighed the mountains in scales, and the hills in a balance?" (Isaiah 40. 12-22). "He causeth the grass to grow for the cattle, and herb for the service of man, that he may bring forth food out of the earth." (Psalm 104. 9-33). "Shall I lift up mine eyes unto the hills: whence should my help come? My help cometh from the Lord which made heaven and earth. He will not suffer thy foot to be moved: He that keeps thee will not slumber. The Lord shall preserve thy going out and thy coming in from this time forth and even for evermore" (Psalm 121).

His greatness is seen equally in the vast and in the minute; in the exquisite lustre which He gives to an insect's wing, and in those countless orbs which are held in position by His power.

> "Not a flower
> But shows some touch in freckle, streak, or stain,
> Of His unrivalled pencil. He inspires
> Their balmy odours and imparts their hues,
> And bathes their eyes with nectar, and includes
> In grains as countless as the seaside sands
> The forms with which He sprinkles all the earth.
> Happy who walks with Him; whom, what he finds
> Of flavour or of scent in fruit or flower,
> Or what he views of beautiful or grand
> In nature, from the broad majestic oak
> To the green blade that twinkles in the sun,
> Prompts with remembrance of a present God."

And this God—now finally revealed to us in Christ— "this God is our God forever and ever; He will be our guide even unto death " (Psalm 48. 14).

CHAPTER THREE

TERMS USED IN GENESIS I

1. FOREGLEAMS OF THE TRINITY

IN the Hebrew language there are three numbers: singular, one; dual, two; plural, more than two. The word for God in Genesis 1.1 is in the plural—indicating at least three persons; but the verb "created" to which it is grammatically joined is in the singular—clearly conveying the idea of the trinity and unity of the Godhead. We have here, then, the first foregleam of what is so fully unfolded later on namely, that "there are three that bear record in heaven, the Father, the Word, and the Holy Ghost; and these three are one" (1 John 5. 7). You have the Father in Genesis 1. 1; the Spirit in verse 2; and the Word (God said) in verse 3 (compare John 1. 1).

There are other indications of this great truth in the book of Genesis. "Let *us* make man" (Genesis 1. 26)—there is plurality; "God created man in *His* own image" (Genesis 1. 27)—there is unity. See also Genesis 3. 22, "The Lord God said, behold the man is become as one of us." "The Lord said . . . let us go down" (Genesis 11. 6-7).

2. THE HEAVENS

There is a threefold division of the celestial region.

(a) The atmospheric heavens from which the rains come (Genesis 8. 2), through which the winds blow (Daniel 8. 8), in which the birds fly (Daniel 2. 38).

(b) The stellar heavens in which are those innumerable orbs of light which, with the sun and moon, men have erroneously worshipped (Genesis 22. 17; Deuteronomy 17. 3).

(c) The Heaven of heavens—the dwelling place of God

18

(Deuteronomy 10. 14; Psalm 11. 4; Isaiah 66. 1).   Our Father is there (Matthew 6. 9).   Our Saviour is there (Hebrews 4. 14; 9. 24).   By and by we shall be there (John 14. 2-3).   Paul was caught up there (2 Corinthians 12. 2).

3.   "CREATED" . . . "MADE"

These two words occur several times in Genesis 1, and careful examination of the way in which they are used by the divine penman will elucidate many difficulties.

"Created"

The word translated "created" means to bring into existence out of nothing.   It is a word which is never applied to the work of man, and it occurs in Genesis 1 on three occasions only.   It is used:

(a) To describe that act of God by which the material universe came into being (verse 1);

(b) To describe the divine power by which animal life was brought into existence (verse 21); and

(c) To describe the origin of man (verse 27).

It is a remarkable fact that these are precisely the points at which nature has said to science: "thus far and no further."   "All the powers of modern science have failed to originate matter; they have failed to bridge the chasm which separates the living from the non-living; they have failed to bridge the gulf which separates the animal creation from man."

(a) The Origin of Matter.

"In the beginning God created the heaven and the earth" (Genesis 1. 1).   "He spake and it was done; He commanded, and it stood fast" (Psalm 33. 6-9).

(b) The Origin of Life.

The second occasion on which the word is used is at the origin of life: "God created great whales, and every living creature that moveth" (verse 21). Scientists have laboured to prove that life can be spontaneously generated; but in the threefold testimony which follows, we have the conclusions at which, after innumerable experiments, they have arrived.

"So far as science can settle anything this question is settled. The attempt to get the living out of the dead has failed. Spontaneous generation has had to be given up."—(DRUMMOND).

"I affirm that no shred of trustworthy experimental testimony exists to prove that life in our day has ever appeared independently of antecedent life."—(TYNDALL).

"It is established beyond the possibility of doubt that life has no other origin than life itself."—(PROF. VIRCHOW, of Berlin before the Medical Congress at Moscow).

(c) The Origin of Man.

The only other occasion in this chapter on which this word is used is at the creation of man: "God created man in His own image, in the image of God created He him, male and female created He them" (verse 27). Three times in this verse the Spirit of God uses the word "created" as if to insist with all possible emphasis that man is a distinct and independent creation of God. So momentous was the occasion that it was preceded by a council in the Trinity (verse 26: Let us make man); and so marvellous the result, that man is declared to have been created in the very image of God (verse 27). He was from the beginning endowed with capacity for fellowship with his God; and with such intelligence and powers of speech that he could give names to the beasts of the field and the fowls of the air which were brought to him for this purpose (chapter 2. 19-20). The philosophers are talking about the ascent of man, but the truth in this matter is with the poet who, speaking of Adam, says that

> "With him his noblest sons might not compare
> In God-like feature or majestic air;
> Not out of weakness rose his gradual frame,
> Perfect from his Creator's hand he came:
> And as in form excelling, so in mind,
> The sire of man transcended all mankind."

"Made"

The word translated "made" (verses 7, 16) means to fashion out of existing material. Thus a carpenter might *make* a table in six days—that is, fashion it out of existing material; but he could not create it. You will now see a new meaning in Exodus 20. 11: "In six days the Lord made—that is, fashioned out of material already existing —the earthly home of man."

4. THE WORD "DAY"

The word "Day" is sometimes used in Scripture to denote a lengthened period. Thus "the day of salvation" (2 Corinthians 6. 2) has already lasted for nearly twenty centuries; "the day of temptation in the wilderness" (Psalm 95. 8) lasted for forty years (verse 10). But when, as in Genesis 1, this word has a numeral attached to it, the meaning is thereby restricted to 24 hours (see carefully Genesis 8. 3; Jonah 1. 17; 3. 4; Acts 1. 3). The Scripture which seems conclusive on this matter is Exodus 20. 8-11, in which "we have the fourth commandment concerning the Sabbath, wherein we have the seven days of the week, and the seven days of reconstruction put together without one word of differentiation between the respective days. We could only assert that the one set of days was entirely different from the other if clear proof were forthcoming from other parts of Scripture, and it is not."

5. "AFTER HIS KIND"

"Evolution declares that life originated in a primordial germ, a protoplasmic cell, living but structureless. From this microscopic beginning life developed by the principle of evolution along the lines of heredity, natural selection, adaptation to environment and the struggle for existence, from lower to higher powers of life, from these to higher still, till ultimately it culminated in man."

"While many superior minds have adopted this theory,

yet many candid and sober scientific teachers maintain that it is a mere hypothesis, lacking any complete or satisfactory scientific demonstration and contradicted by some of the most inexorable facts of physiology; especially this cardinal and insurmountable difficulty that even in the present orders of the animal world, it is certain that species do not blend and propagate a new species, but that such unions always terminate with the second link, and leave it without the power of reproduction."

The expression "after his kind" which occurs ten times in Genesis 1 gives the deathblow to the theory of evolution. For while there was imparted to each species the power of reproduction—"whose seed was in itself"—there is not the slightest hint in Scripture, there is not a single proof in nature, that lower species develop into higher species. Throughout the entire historical periods monkeys have been monkeys; they are precisely the same creatures they were three thousand years ago in Egypt ,and five thousand years ago in Babylonia. "In all that great museum," said Robert Etheridge, head of the geological department of the British Museum, "in all that great museum there is not a particle of evidence of transmutation of species. Nine-tenths of the talk of evolutionists is not founded on observation, and is wholly unsupported by facts. This museum is full of proofs of the utter falsity of their views." The Scripture makes it clear that in each case God's intervention was direct; and the language used is so unmistakable that you cannot accept the theory of Evolution without first repudiating the Word of God.

My brother, hold fast to your ancestors in the garden of Eden; let those who will, trace theirs to the Zoological gardens.

6. "IMAGE" . . . "LIKENESS"

"Image" has reference to the position in which man was placed: he represented God as governor over all His creatures. Man's dominion extended over the fish of the

sea, and over the fowl of the air, and over everything
that moveth upon the earth (Genesis 1. 28; Psalm 8);
and reference to the life of God's ideal Man—the man
Christ Jesus—will show how beneficially that dominion
could have been exercised. The fowls of the air were
represented by a dove when Heaven testified to its delight
in Him (Matthew 3. 16); the fish of the sea brought a
piece of money at His command (Matthew 17. 27); the
beast of the field provided an ass for Him to ride upon
(Matthew 21. 2). He lived unharmed among the wild
beasts (Mark 1. 13).

Sin has, however, destroyed man's supremacy in the
earth, and the Edenic covenant of dominion has given
place to the Noachian covenant of dread (Genesis 9. 2).
The animal creation no longer owns his sway, and their
defiance of him will continue until the time so graphically
described in Isaiah 11. 6-9 when

> "The lion and the leopard and the bear
>   Shall graze with the fearless flocks. All bask
>   At noon together, or all gambol in the shade
>   Of the same grove, or drink one common stream.
>   Antipathies are none.   No foe to man
>   Lurks in the serpent now: the mother sees,
>   And smiles to see, her infant's playful hand
>   Stretched forth to dally with the crested worm;
>   To stroke his azure back, or to receive
>   The lambent homage of his arrowy tongue.
>   All creatures worship man, and all mankind
>   One Lord one Father."

If "Image" has to do with man's position in that he
represented God, "Likeness" has to do with his nature in
that he resembled God.   He was free from all taint of sin;
he was pure and spotless, and in this he was like God.
By the Fall that likeness was lost, and so the Bible speaks
of three types of humanity:

1. Adam's, which was innocent (Genesis 1. 27).
2. Ours, which is sinful (Psalm 51. 5).
3. Christ's, which was holy (Luke 1. 35).

Our likeness to God will be restored when we shall see Him as He is (1 John 3. 2); and then, and only then, will the renewed heart be fully and finally satisfied (Psalm 17. 15).

7. THE SABBATH (GENESIS 2. 1-3)

The institution and sanctification of the Sabbath—that is, the setting apart of one day in seven for rest and for sacred uses—dates from the days of Adam, and clearly indicates what our Lord subsequently declared, namely, that the Sabbath was made for man, and not merely for a nation (Mark 2. 27). Indeed, seven is stamped on the constitution of nature. The human body undergoes renewal every seven years; fevers run their course by seven day periods—the pulse lowers its record one day in seven; there are seven prismatic colours in light; there are seven notes in a musical scale. And the observance of this law of rest—which is a merciful one for man and beast—will inevitably bring physical blessing in its train.

One of the larger cities of Scotland is supplied with water from a lake so far up in the hills that, were the water to be brought down in one continuous closed conduit, the pressure of the water at its foot would burst any pipe that man could devise. A great engineer solved the problem by locating small open reservoirs at intervals all the way down, at each one of which the pressure of the water in the pipe was relieved. At no point could the water exceed the weight of the water between that point and the next reservoir above, and it was not hard to find piping strong enough for such a degree of pressure.

What the reservoirs did in breaking the pressure of the water at intervals, the weekly day of rest does for us in relieving at intervals the accumulated strain of business and domestic and social cares. We come out from the pressure of the week before into its quiet hours, and from them start refreshed in body and mind into the strain of the week's duties ahead. The man who habitually breaks his labour by such regular intervals of rest will not easily be driven by the press of business to the point of breaking down.

Looking at this matter from the spiritual point of view we find from the New Testament that "the Sabbath was abolished at the Cross and the Lord's day—the first day of the week—set apart by the Resurrection; that the last-named day was observed by the early Christians as the day of rest from earthly toil, and of assembling for worship and service" (Acts 20). It was on the first day of the week that the Lord Jesus rose from the dead (John 20), that the Holy Spirit descended from Heaven (Acts 2), and that the seer of Patmos received the visions of the Apocalypse (Revelation 1). The spiritual teaching which underlies these facts is very beautiful. Under Law the people toiled six days and rested on the seventh—that is to say, rest was the goal. Under Grace, we rest on the first day of the week and work during the other six—that is to say, rest is the starting-point.

Chapter Four

THE TYPICAL TEACHING OF GENESIS 1

IN Second Corinthians 5. 17 Paul declares that "if any man be in Christ there is a new creation" (R.V.); and in chapter 4. 6 of the same epistle, that "God Who commanded the light to shine out of darkness, hath shined in our hearts, to give the light of the knowledge of the glory of God in the face of Jesus Christ." By so doing, he clearly implies that the original creation of Genesis 1. 1, the chaos into which it subsequently fell (Genesis 1. 2), and the various stages of the reconstruction of the ruined earth (Genesis 1. 3-31) are all typical of greater things. We propose now to trace the six days work recorded in our chapter, and to point out how marvellously they foreshadow the stages by which the life divine is developed in the soul of man.

(1) "In the beginning God created the heaven and the earth"; and He created them, as He usually does things —with divine and absolute perfection. Reason would expect this to be so; Scripture assures us that it was so (Isaiah 45. 18).

What God did for creation He did for man. "God made man upright" (Ecclesiastes 7. 29). The Creator made him pure, intellectual, kingly, Godlike—a being who could hold fellowship with Him, and with whom He could converse.

(2) But, as we have already seen, at some time and for some reason not fully revealed, the perfect creation became a ruin. "The earth became waste and void and darkness was upon the face of the deep."

The desolation which came upon the material creation is a striking figure of the moral chaos which, because of sin, came upon man. The unregenerate heart is a scene of dark disorder and spiritual death; no words could more fittingly describe it than those in verse 2—formless, empty, dark. One eminent preacher, conscious of the plague of his own heart, who was urged by the exponents of the new school to give up the old truths, replied in the following pathetic words:

> "From bondage to the old beliefs
> You say, our rescue must begin;
> But I—need refuge from my griefs
> And cleansing from my sin.
>
> The strong, the easy, and the glad
> Hang blandly listening on your word,
> But I—am sick, and I—am sad,
> And I need Thee, O Lord."

(3) And now, just as God took the shapeless ruin—which was the wreck of the primeval order—and fashioned it into a thing of beauty and order and life; so does He take up man and, by processes which are altogether divine, transforms him from a condition of moral chaos into one of spiritual beauty, and from one which is characterised by darkness and death into one which is characterised by light and life. But let us see how this comes about.

(4) DAY 1. "The Spirit of God moved upon the face of the waters." And God said: "Let there be light and there was light" (verses 2-3). Here then is the beginning of the reconstruction of the ruined earth, and it is a perfect picture of the beginning of the divine life in the soul. The Spirit of God moved, and God said—that is, the Spirit and the Word—precisely the two agents employed in the regeneration of fallen man. We are born again of the Spirit (John 3. 5) and by the Word (1 Peter 1.23).

The result of the action of the Spirit and the Word is light; and the first thing the light shines upon is the ruin. It is for this reason that the first consequence of faithful gospel preaching is that sacred sorrow which worketh repentance to salvation not to be repented of (2 Corinthians

7. 10); for the light reveals the ruin which sin has caused·
But just as repentance—which is the tear drop in the eye
of faith—becomes the harbinger of ultimate joy, so the
light which reveals to us what we are, reveals to us also
what God is: it gives the knowledge of the glory of God in
the face of Jesus Christ (2 Corinthians 4. 6).

"And God called the light day and the darkness He
called night" (verse 5). These two material symbols—
darkness and light—are constantly employed in later
portions of God's Word to illustrate spiritual realities.
Thus Paul tells the Ephesian Christians that they were
sometimes darkness, but now they were light in the Lord
(Ephesians 5. 8); Peter reminds those to whom he writes
that they were called out of darkness into His marvellous
light (1 Peter 2. 9); and, because we are thus the children
of light and the children of the day (1 Thess. 5. 5) we are
to cast off the works of darkness, and put on the armour
of light (Romans 13. 12).

"The evening and the morning were the first day"
(verse 5). The order is from darkness to light.

(5) DAY 2. "And God said, Let there be a firmament
in the midst of the waters, and let it divide the waters
from the waters . . . and it was so" (verse 6-8). If light
is the first experience in the new life, division or separation
is its first practical result. So has it ever been. The first
great event after the slaying of the passover lamb by which
the Israelites were redeemed was the crossing of the Red
Sea. That mighty sea opened in front of them to let
them out of Egypt, and closed behind them to keep them
out. In antitypical language, the cross which delivers us
from the world stands between us and the world (Galatians
6. 14).

(6) DAY 3. Verses 9 to 13. There are two commands
here, and the first is: "Let the dry land appear." At the
divine decree the waters receded, the earth was liberated,

and rose from the watery grave in which it had been submerged (Psalm 104. 6-9).

The third day is resurrection day and is constantly spoken of as such (Matthew 16. 21; 17. 22-23; 20. 18-19; Acts 10. 39-40). Just as in God's reckoning the believer was crucified with Christ (Galatians 2. 20), so is he also reckoned to have risen with Him (Colossians 2. 12; 3. 1). The supreme fact in the earthly life of our Lord becomes thus the supreme factor in ours; and when we enter into the living power of this great truth (Philippians 3. 10) we shall indeed stand fast in the liberty wherewith Christ has made us free (Galatians 5. 1).

> "Buried with Christ and raised with Him too,
> What is there left for me to do?
> Simply to cease from struggling and strife,
> Simply to walk in newness of life."

The second command is: "Let the earth bring forth . . . fruit" (verse 11). As the resurrected earth was commanded to put on her robes of verdure and beauty so are we commanded to put on ours. The same chapter that tells us we are risen with Christ bids us to put on as the elect of God, holy and beloved, a heart of compassion, kindness, humbleness of mind, meekness, longsuffering . . . and above all these things put on love which is the bond of perfectness (compare Colossians 3. 1, 12-14).

(7) DAY 4. Sun: Moon: Stars (verses 14-19). Our eyes are now directed to the heavens and we are told of the appointment of sun, moon, and stars "to give light upon the earth" (verse 15).

The sun prefigures the Lord Jesus Who is spoken of as "the Sun of righteousness" (Malachi 4. 2) and Who spoke of Himself as the Light of the world (John 8. 12). The moon is a figure of the church collectively; while the stars represent believers individually (Daniel 12. 3).

"He telleth the number of the stars; He calleth them all by their names" (Psalm 147. 4). That is a word for you, young Christian. He knows your name (John 10. 3, 27), the city in which you reside (Acts 18. 10), the street in which you dwell (Acts 9. 11) the very house in which you live (Acts 10. 6), and is intimately acquainted with all your ways (Psalm 139. 1-10). May your life be a bright and shining witness for Him, and be used by Him to bring many to the knowledge of Himself. "He that winneth souls is wise" (Proverbs 11. 30) and "they that be wise shall shine as the brightness of the firmament, and they that turn many to righteousness as the stars for ever and ever" (Daniel 12. 3).

(8) DAY 5. Verses 20-23. The aerial and aquatic regions are now peopled with fowl and fish respectively; and the word "abundantly" is twice used to describe the overflowing measure of life with which those regions were blessed. "God said: let the waters bring forth abundantly the moving creature that hath life, and fowl that they may fly above the earth in the open firmament of heaven" (verse 20). It is a picture of the life which the Lord Jesus came to impart. "I am come that they might have life, and that they might have it more abundantly" (John 10. 10). The fishes are equipped with fins to move through the waters, and with scales to resist the action of the waters; the eagle can mount up on wings and gaze undazzled on the sun—figures these, of the power which enables the believer to press on through the hostile element by which he is surrounded (Philippians 3. 7-14); of the grace that keeps him from the evil which is in the world (John 17. 15); and of the heavenly life which becomes ours as we wait on the Lord (Isaiah 40. 31).

(9) DAY 6. "So God created man in His Own image, in the image of God created He him; male and female created He them" (verse 27). This is the outstanding event of the sixth day, and by it the first creation was completed and crowned.

The new creation similarly reaches its climax in "the new man which is renewed in knowledge after the image of Him that created him" (Colossians 3. 10). This process is going on now, (2 Corinthians 3. 18); it will be completed when we stand in His presence (Romans 8. 29). "As we have borne the image of the earthy, we shall also bear the image of the heavenly" (1 Corinthians 15. 49).

(10) DAY 7. The Sabbath—ch. 2. 1-3. "God rested on the seventh day from all His work which He made; and God blessed the seventh day and hallowed it." Just as the creation process culminated in rest, so also does the redemptive process. "The Lord thy God in the midst of thee is mighty; He will save, He will rejoice over thee with joy; He will rest in His love, He will joy over thee with singing" (Zephaniah 3. 17).

Summary

Day 1.   Light.
Day 2.   Separation.
Day 3.   Resurrection.
Day 4.   Witnessing.
Day 5.   Abundant Life.
Day 6.   Image of God.
Day 7.   Rest.

CHAPTER FIVE

MAN—GENESIS 2

FROM the story of creation as a whole which we have in Genesis 1, we pass, in chapter 2, to consider in detail one separate portion of it—the story of man. It has been said that these two accounts, so far as they relate to the creation of man, are contradictory; but that statement is incorrect. They are complementary but not contradictory. In the first chapter the creation of man is set forth as the consummating glory of the handiwork of God (Psalm 139. 14); in the second chapter that event constitutes the starting point in human history. In the former, the fact of his creation is declared; in the latter, the process of his formation is described. Genesis 1 resembles the map of Palestine which you find at the end of your Bibles; Genesis 2 corresponds to the inset which describes in detail a portion of that country—Jerusalem and its environs.

In this connection these two chapters form a splendid illustration of a law, the recognition of which is essential to all intelligent Bible study: I mean the law of recurrence. Dr. Gray defines it as "that peculiarity of the Holy Spirit as an author by which He gives first the outlines of a subject and then recurs to it for the purpose of adding details." Thus, as we have seen in Genesis 1. 27 the fact of the creation of man is announced; in chapter 2 the Spirit returns to the theme and describes separately and in detail the creation of man (verse 7) and of woman (verses 21-22).

Take another instance. In Numbers 13. 1-2 we read that "the Lord spake unto Moses saying: send thou men that they may search the land of Canaan which I give unto the children of Israel; of every tribe of their fathers shall ye send a man," which conveys the impression that the thought of sending spies into Canaan originated with the Lord. When, however, we turn to Deuteronomy 1. 22, we find that the suggestion came from the people. "Ye came near unto me" said Moses, "ye came near unto me every one of you and said: we will send men before us and they shall search us out the land, and bring us word again." The sending of the spies was the fruit of unbelief; but if we had not the added truth of Deuteronomy 1. 22, we should not have known this.

Or take the story of Lot. If we had only the record in Genesis, this man would stand before us without a single redeeming feature. But when we turn to 2 Peter, 2. 7-8, we find the Spirit of God laying bare his inner history. He speaks of him as "just Lot—that righteous man" and tells us that he vexed his righteous soul from day to day because of the unlawful deeds of the people of that guilty city.

There is one supreme exception to this law; and that is where God deals with the sins of His people. For example: the second book of Samuel which records the historical facts, exposes the terrible sin of David (2 Samuel 11); the first book of Chronicles which covers the same historical ground but which gives God's thoughts about these facts makes no mention of that sin. For David had confessed his sin with bitter tears; and God's messenger had assured him that the Lord had put it away (Psalm 51; 2 Samuel 12. 13).

So also in Hebrews 11. 29-30 the historian passes from the crossing of the Red Sea to the falling down of the walls of Jericho, and makes no mention of the forty years of rebellion and wandering which lay between these two events. For God had declared in the previous chapter (Hebrews 10. 17) that their sins and iniquities He would remember no more.

The important lesson which we learn from the existence of this law is, that in order to know the mind of God on any matter which is dealt with in His Word we must examine all that is said about it in that Word. But remember also that the silences of Scripture are as much inspired as are its statements.

Elohim: Jehovah

You will have observed that in the first section of Genesis (chapter 1. 1 to 2. 3) the title "God" is used, and that chapter 2. 4 to verse 25 uses a different title—"the Lord God". The word "God" is the English translation of the Hebrew "Elohim"; the words "Lord God" are the translation of the Hebrew words "Jehovah Elohim." These two names of Deity are used throughout the Bible with absolute precision and discrimination.

Elohim—usually translated "God"—is the creatorial name of Deity; Jehovah—usually translated "Lord"—is the redemption name of Deity. Or, as Dr. Gray has said: Elohim is His far-off name; Jehovah is His near-by name. Thus in Genesis 1 you are surrounded by the evidences of might, power, and Godhead, and hence in that chapter you find 32 times the word which describes the Creator from that point of view—Elohim. In Genesis 2 you have the Creator in covenant relationship with man; and hence you find there 11 times the words which describe that— Jehovah Elohim.

In later portions of Scripture where these two names are used in relationship to the affairs of men, Jehovah is employed when His covenant people are concerned; and Elohim when He is dealing with those who know Him not. I quote from a writer who gives three instances out of many in which this distinction is very strikingly presented.

(1) "And they that went in, went in male and female of all flesh as God (Elohim) had commanded him; and the Lord (Jehovah) shut him in" (Genesis 7. 16). Elohim was going to destroy the world which He had made, but Jehovah took care of the man with whom He stood in relation.

(2) "That all the earth may know that there is a God (Elohim) in Israel. And all this assembly shall know that the Lord (Jehovah) saveth not with sword and spear" (1 Samuel 17. 46-47). All the earth was to recognise the presence of Elohim but Israel was called to recognise the actings of Jehovah with Whom they stood in relation.

(3) "Jehoshaphat cried out and the Lord (Jehovah) helped him; and God (Elohim) moved them to depart from him" (2 Chronicles 18. 31). Jehovah took care of His poor erring servant; but Elohim, though unknown, acted upon the hearts of the uncircumcised Syrians.

These two titles finally appear in the two closing chapters of Inspiration which treat of redeemed man and a new earth.

*   *   *   *

The second chapter of Genesis tells the story of man; and there are four things relative to him which are to engage our attention.

(1) THE PROCESS BY WHICH HE WAS FORMED (VERSE 7)

"And the Lord God formed man of the dust of the ground, and breathed into his nostrils the breath of life; and man became a living soul." This is a most important Scripture; for, taken in conjunction with Genesis 1. 27, 1 Thess. 5. 23, and Hebrews 4. 12, it places in our hand the key which unlocks the door into Biblical psychology. God first moulded the inanimate frame and then breathed into it the breath of lives—that is to say, there was a combination of the material and the spiritual. When we examine the words of 1 Thess. 5. 23 we find that the integral parts of a man's being are three in number; that he is composed of spirit, and soul, and body.

(a) The spirit is the highest and noblest part of him. It is that by means of which we are able to apprehend God and to worship Him. Dr. Pierson strikingly compares it to a lofty observatory from which it was possible to explore the unseen world and the realm of spiritual realities. He goes on to say that since the Fall, the spirit of man has become like a dismantled observatory which, with its apparatus for studying the heavens, has been wrecked by an earthquake. The same brilliant writer uses another simile which is even more striking. He says that the spirit of fallen man is like the holy of holies in the Tabernacle or Temple forsaken of the divine presence, and with the divine uncreated Shekinah fire quenched, leaving it in midnight darkness. Regeneration is the rekindling of that quenched Shekinah flame. It is the introduction of life into the death chamber, of light into the darkness. And hence it is that while from the wise and prudent of this world the Father has withheld the revelation of His higher truths, He has revealed them unto babes; those born again in the image of His Son and endowed with the seeing eye (Matthew 11. 25-27).

(b) The soul is the seat of the intellectual and emotional faculties, giving us capacity for fellowship with our fellow-men. It includes mental perception, imagination, memory, and natural affection (1 Sam. 18. 1).

(c) The body gives us the use of the five senses—sight, hearing, taste, touch, and smell—which Bunyan represents as the five avenues or gates to the city of Mansoul. It stands related to the spirit as the tenement to the tenant.

A clear apprehension of these distinctions will enable us to understand many parts of Scripture, for upon the threefold nature of man a number of New Testament exhortations are founded. It will also help us to grasp more intelligently some aspects of truth that bear on the temptation and fall of man, and on the nature of spiritual death.

It should be carefully noted that each part of our nature can be satisfied only with the nourishment which is suited to it. "The body has its appropriate nutriment and sustenance—it is found in air and food; and its highest welfare is reached through good physical habits of exercise and cleanliness. The soul has its own sustenance and satisfaction; it feeds on thought, knowledge, learning, literature, art, human enterprise, and natural affection. But the spirit has both higher wants and capacities. It yearns after knowledge of God and fellowship with Him, verifying thus the ancient word of Augustine: "Thou hast made us for Thyself, O God, and we are restless till we rest in Thee."

To sum up: The spirit is the seat of our God-consciousness (Romans 8. 16); the soul is the seat of our self-consciousness (Psalm 43. 5); the body is the seat of our world-consciousness (2 Cor. 5. 1).

(2) THE HOME IN WHICH HE WAS PLACED (VERSES 8-15)

The exact locality of man's original home has been the subject of much discussion. Those who are competent to discuss such a question on other than Scriptural grounds agree with the Biblical narrative that the cradle of mankind is to be looked for somewhere in the country watered by the Tigris and the Euphrates. Sir William Dawson, for example, was convinced that, geologically, that district is the only spot upon which man could have lived at the first; and it is noteworthy that the region of the Euphrates is the native home of the cereals which formed man's original food (Genesis 1. 29).

It has been pointed out that in Genesis 2 we have all that is ordinarily necessary to the growth of plants and herbs: soil, climate, culture. We have first the vital energy of the earth itself in which all seeds are lodged (verse 5); secondly, heaven's genial moisture (verse 6); and thirdly, man's faithful husbandry (verses 7-15).

Everything that grew in Eden was either beautiful or useful (verse 9). It was indeed "a scene of pre-eminent beauty and superabounding delights."

Here then in a perfect environment man was placed with the sceptre of dominion in his hand (Psalm 8. 6-9). That dominion—which lasted until sin entered into the world—extended over the five great regions of animate and inanimate nature as described in Genesis 1. 26; and in Genesis 2. 19-20 we find Adam exercising the prerogatives with which that sovereignty invested him. It seems clear from the two last named verses that language was a gift direct from Heaven. Man's first recorded act was the naming of the beasts and birds brought to him for this purpose. Nouns—names—are the rudiments of speech.

It should be carefully noted that the claim made by spiritists that we may cross the boundaries laid down in Genesis 1. 26 into the unseen world is not only destitute of authority, but is elsewhere in the book of God most sternly forbidden (Deuteronomy 18. 10-12). Our lunatic asylums bear terrible witness to the awful results which flow from attempts to do this. As you value your physical, mental, and spiritual health and well-being, touch not this unclean thing.

(3) THE PROHIBITION BY WHICH HE WAS TESTED (VERSES 16-17)

These verses describe the bountifulness of the creator God. There was no restriction placed upon Adam except one simple test of obedience which involved no sacrifice of happiness and no question of love. There was the maximum of liberty and the minimum of prohibition. One thing, and one thing only, he was not to do (verse 17).

Sceptics have said a great deal about the triviality of the prohibition, and the terrible consequences which flowed from disobedience to it; but all such talk is beside the mark. If Adam was to be tried at all it could scarcely be otherwise than by a positive precept. "If it be asked why God did not create a man who could not sin, the answer must be: because He made a man."

"In the day thou eatest thereof thou shalt surely die." "This," says Dr. Parker, "this is not a threat. It is not a defiance or a challenge. It is a revelation; it is a warning. When you tell your child not to touch the fire or it will be burned, you do not threaten the child, you warn it in love, and solely for its own good. Foolish would the child be, if it asked why there should be any fire; and foolish are we, with high aggravations, when we ask why God should have set the tree of life and the tree of knowledge in Eden."

"The tree of death (Genesis 2. 17) appears at the beginning of the Bible; the tree of Calvary (1 Peter 2. 24) appears in the middle of the Bible; and the tree of life (Revelation 2. 7) appears at the end of the Bible."

(4) The Companion with Whom he was Favoured (Verses 18-25)

In verse 18 we have a revelation of the kindness of God to His creature man in that He provided him with an helpmeet—one who would share his joys, his purposes, and his enterprises. And then in verses 21-24 we have the details of her formation. Of this event Matthew Henry says that "when God made woman He did not take her out of man's head to lord it over him, nor out of his feet to be trampled on by him, but out of his side to be equal with him, from under his arm to be protected by him, from near his heart to be loved by him." Adam thus met with his superior in the Creator, with his inferiors in the animals, and with his equal in Eve.

"An helpmeet." Washington Irving has compared such a woman to the vine. "As the vine, which has long twined its graceful foliage about the oak, and been lifted by it into sunshine will, when the hardy plant is rifted by the thunderbolt, cling round it with its caressing tendrils, and bind up its shattered boughs; so it is beautifully ordered by Providence that woman should be man's stay and solace when smitten with sudden calamity, binding up the broken heart."

CHAPTER SIX

GENESIS AND REVELATION

"THE Bible as a whole" says Professor Dyson Hague, "is like a chain hanging upon two staples. The book of Genesis is the one staple, the book of Revelation is the other. Take away either staple and the chain falls in confusion. If the first chapters of Genesis are unreliable, the revelation of the beginning of the universe, the origin of the race, and the reason for its redemption are gone. If the last chapters of the Revelation are displaced, the consummation of all things is unknown. If you take away Genesis, you have lost the explanation of the first heaven, the first earth, the first Adam and the Fall. If you take away Revelation you have lost the completed truth of the new heaven, and the new earth, man redeemed, and the last Adam in paradise regained."

Genesis—which is the preface to the entire Bible—thus unveils to us the dateless and otherwise unknown past; Revelation—which is the conclusion to the Bible—tells of the dateless and otherwise unknown future. The first two chapters of the one show us what man was before sin entered into the world; the two closing chapters of the other describe what he will become after sin shall have forever passed away. Between these two extreme points—that is to say, from Genesis 3 to Revelation 20—the Word of God gives a full description of the conflict of the ages; of the painful journey which the redeemed take as they travel from the earthly paradise lost through sin, to the paradise of God attained by grace divine.

During the period of time covered by these last named records, three things are in evidence wherever man is found—sin, sorrow, death. Let those who deny the historicity of Genesis chapter three explain these things if they can.

I propose now to place side by side from these earliest and latest chapters of the book of God statements which correspond to each other; and these will refer to the three great themes of which they treat, namely, to Creation, to Man, and to Satan.

1. IN RELATION TO CREATION

GENESIS		REVELATION	
(a) Cursed	Chap. 3. 17.	No more curse	Chap. 22. 3.
(b) Sun govern day	,, 1. 16.	No need of sun	,, 22. 5.
(c) Darkness night	,, 1. 2.	No night there	,, 22. 5.
(d) Paradise of man,	,, 2. 15.	Paradise of God	,, 2. 7.

These verses from the book of Revelation reveal the one grand event to which the whole creation moves (Romans 8. 20-22 R.V.). Deeply significant, is it not, that the crown which they placed on the Saviour's brow was a crown of thorns—the emblem of the curse (Genesis 3. 17, 18; Matthew 27. 29). He lifted the curse; was made a curse for us (Galatians 3. 13).

Observe that what was dust in the first paradise, is gold in the second; and that while the first was in the corner of a small planet, the second is a universe of glory in which nations dwell.

From time immemorial men have spoken of the good days of old, and of the good days to come, and with a wistfulness that reminds one of the sea-shell on the mantelshelf sighing for its ocean home. The memory of the past is explained in the book of Genesis; the hope of the future is assured in the book of Revelation.

2. IN RELATION TO MAN

GENESIS		REVELATION	
(a) Sorrow	Chap. 3. 16-17.	No more sorrow	Chap. 21. 4.
(b) Burdensome toil,	,, 3. 19.	Unwearied service	,, 22. 3.
(c) Death	,, 3. 19.	No more death	,, 21. 4.
(d) Banished	,, 3. 24.	Welcomed home	,, 21. 3.

Have you noticed that Heaven and our Inheritance are described mostly by negatives? (compare 1 Peter 1. and Revelation chapters 21 and 22). It would seem that human language is incapable of fully conveying to us what will be there; and hence the Spirit of God points to the things with which we are so tragically familiar here —sorrow, pain, defilement, decay, death—and assures us that these will not be there.

3. IN RELATION TO SATAN

GENESIS				REVELATION	
(a) Deceiving	Chap. 3.	1-4.	No more	Chap. 20.	3
(b) Doom pronounced	3.	15.	Doom executed	,, 20.	10.

May not this exposure of Satan's history and doom be the explanation of the malignity with which, through the ages, he has attacked these two great books of Scripture? He would persuade man that the one is all myth and the other all mystery and so rob them of the warning and encouragement which they unitedly present. But we are not ignorant of his devices.

Chapter Seven

THE FALL AND ITS CONSEQUENCES (1)

THE third chapter of Genesis forms the pivot of the Bible. If it be not a record of historical facts, then some of the deepest things of life must remain insoluble mysteries. The tendency of human nature to degenerate, the universality and persistency of evil in the world, the fact that right is so frequently on the scaffold and wrong so frequently on the throne—all these things imply that some grave moral catastrophe has overtaken the human race; and I affirm that we have no adequate explanation of it save that which is given in the chapter now before us. Not only so: cut this chapter out of your Bible and the remainder of it becomes meaningless: it will be like "a splendid edifice without a foundation, a gorgeous castle hanging in the air."

1. THE TEMPTATION (VERSES 1-5)

"Now the serpent ... said unto the woman: 'Yea hath, God said, ye shall not eat of every tree of the garden?'" (verse 1).

The fact that when the serpent spoke to her, Eve was not surprised, seems clearly to indicate that before the Fall there was some intelligent means of communication between man and the animal creation over which he reigned. Nor, as Dr. Schofield has pointed out, is the serpent in his Edenic form to be thought of as the venomous reptile which we know to-day. His degradation was the result of the curse pronounced upon him, prior to which he held himself upright—the most subtle and probably the most beautiful of all the beasts of the field (verse 4). Traces of that beauty remain to this day despite the curse; every movement is graceful and some species are beautifully coloured.

From later portions of God's Word, however, we learn
that the serpent was merely the tool in the hands of a
spiritual personality who aimed at thwarting the purposes
of God, and at robbing man of his blessedness. The New
Testament declares that the temptation was literal (2
Corinthians 11. 3; 1 Timothy 2. 14) and that the real
tempter was the devil—the daring adversary of God, the
merciless enemy of man (Rev. 12. 9; 20. 2).

Carefully observe that Satan uses the title Elohim—
God—which speaks of might, power, and Godhead; and
not Jehovah—Lord—which speaks of covenant relationship and blessing. By so doing, he conveys to the mind
of Eve the impression that God is far away and too great
to have any interest in the creatures whom He has made.
Eve falls into the trap and speaks of her Benefactor and
Friend by the same title (verse 3).

"Yea, hath God said?" There is a law in Scripture
known to Bible students as the law of first mention.
Briefly stated, that law means that the first mention
of a word or a subject in holy writ is the key to its subsequent meanings. "The very first words on any subject
on which the Holy Spirit is going to treat, are the keystone
of the whole matter."

The application of this law to the subject now before
us is most instructive. Here we have the first temptation,
and the first revelation of the tempter and his methods.
"Satan's character and wiles are here disclosed at the
very beginning, and the ground of all failure is seen to be
in questioning the Word of God and not acting in simple
belief of it." The first recorded words of the devil in the
Old Testament cast a doubt on the spoken word of God
(Genesis 3. 1); his first recorded words in the New Testament cast a doubt on the living Word of God (Matthew
4. 3). "Yea, hath God said" was his word to Eve; "if thou
be the Son of God" was his word to the Master—although
the Father had just previously declared: "This is My
beloved Son" (Matthew 3. 17).

It appears, therefore, that the punctuation mark of which the devil is fondest, is the interrogation point (Job 1. 9). And he is using the question mark very freely to-day. Behind the inspiration of the Scriptures, the Incarnation, the Atonement, the Resurrection, and other fundamental truths of Christianity he raises a big question mark. So great and so widespread has been the defection from these verities, that the question which our Lord asked: "when the Son of Man cometh shall He find the faith on the earth?" (Luke 18. 8 R.V.) takes on to-day a significance which it never had before.

The stages by which man's ruin was encompassed are clearly marked. There was:

(a) Doubt of God's goodness (verse 1)

"Is it really true that God has restricted you from the use of every tree in this delightful place? Are you quite sure that you are not mistaken?"

Now notice: when God placed man and woman in the garden He emphasised the liberty with which He invested them. "Of every tree of the garden thou mayest freely eat" save one (chapter 2. 16-17). But when Satan speaks, he conceals the privileges and harps on the single prohibition. Keeping out of sight what God had done for them, the unnumbered gifts and proofs of love everywhere, the serpent fixes on the one thing denied and brings it forward in a way calculated to awaken hard and evil thoughts in the mind of Eve.

(b) Distortion of His Word (verses 2-3)

In the form of Eve's answer, it is plainly manifest that the poison of doubt which the devil injected into her mind is beginning to do its deadly work. She exaggerates the severity of the prohibition, and minimises the danger of transgression. She speaks as if God were a hard master and a lenient judge.

An old servant of Christ set down on one of the pages

of his Bible the threefold principle which guided him in the study of it, namely:

1. Take nothing from it.
2. Add nothing to it.
3. Change nothing in it.

Eve did all three of these.

(1) She took from the Word of God. He had said: "Of every tree of the garden thou mayest freely eat" save one; but Eve omitted the word "freely" thus making God to appear less bountiful than He was (compare Genesis 2. 16; 3. 2). "Ye shall not diminish from the Word which I command you" (Deuteronomy 4. 2).

(2) She added to the Word of God. He had said of the tree of the knowledge of good and evil: "Thou shalt not eat of it." But in her reply to Satan, Eve declared that God had also said: "Neither shall ye touch it" which He had not (Genesis 2. 17; 3. 3). "Add thou not unto His words lest He reprove thee, and thou be found a liar" (Proverbs 30. 6).

(3) She changed the Word of God. He had said: "In the day that thou eatest thereof thou shalt surely die"; but when our first mother quoted the words of warning she said: "neither shall ye touch it *lest* ye die" (Genesis 2. 17; 3. 3) and by doing so changed an absolute certainty into a mere possibility. "Man shall not live by bread alone, but by every word that proceedeth out of the mouth of God" (Matthew 4. 4).

She thus misquoted the terms of the divine permission, overstated the prohibition, and underrated the penalty.

(c) *Denial of His Warning* (*verse* 4)

The next step is a bold denial of the solemn warning which God gave to man. His goodness and love having been questioned, His plain word having been distorted,

His truthfulness is next assailed. "Yes, He has said that, but fear not, ye shall not surely die"—so said this liar from the beginning (John 8. 44). "Beware", says an American preacher, "beware of Bible commentators who are unwilling to take God's words just as they stand. The first commentator of that sort was the devil in the garden of Eden. He proposed only a slight change—just the one word 'not' to be inserted—'ye shall not surely die.' The amendment was accepted and the world was lost."

(d) Deception as to the Consequences (verse 5)

"Ye shall be as gods knowing good and evil." Tennyson says that a lie which is half the truth is ever the blackest of lies; and that is what we have here. By disobedience she came to know good as a forfeited possession, and evil as a purchased bane; to know good without the power to do it, and evil without the power to resist it. She was deceived (1 Timothy 2. 14).

You will notice that the revised version substitutes "God" for "gods" in verse 5, and shows us that nothing short of equality with the Most High was the lure which the adversary dangled before the longing eyes of Eve; that, just as Satan sought to take God's place in the creation above (Isaiah 14. 12-14) so man sought to take His place on the earth (Genesis 3. 5 R.V.). In this connection, Genesis 3 stands in contrast to Phil. 2. In the former, the first Adam aspired to equality with God and was humbled to the dust; in the latter, the second Adam humbled Himself to the death of the cross, and has been exalted to the highest place in the universe of God (Phil. 2. 5-11).

2. THE FALL (VERSES 6-7)

There, then, was the temptation placed before Eve: and we read that "when the woman saw that the tree was good for food, and that it was pleasant to the eyes, and a tree to be desired to make one wise, she took of the fruit thereof and did eat, and gave also unto her husband with her and he did eat." Doubt, distortion, denial, deception —"the confluence of all these streams made such a current as swept the feeble will clean away; and blinded, dazed, and deafened by the roar of the waters, Eve was carried over the falls as a man might be carried over Niagara."

The days of her innocence were now at an end; and the sixth verse reveals the sad fact that she, the tempted, becomes, in turn, the tempter; she gave to her husband and he did eat. In this connection, however, it is important to remember that while Eve was the victim of deception, Adam was not deceived (1 Timothy 2. 14). It would appear that his love for his wife led him deliberately to determine that he would share the consequences of her sin.

After her confidence in God had been undermined the temptation which led to Eve's undoing was of a threefold character. The tree was (1) good for food; (2) pleasant to the eyes; and (3) a tree to be desired to make one wise. And by comparing this with 1 John 2. 16 we learn that this is the representative plan, and these the master principles, by which Satan seeks to ruin every man. "Good for food"—there is the lust of the flesh, the appeal to the physical nature; "pleasant to the eyes"—there is the lust of the eye, the appeal to the aesthetic nature; "tree to be desired to make one wise"—there is the pride of life, the appeal to the intellectual nature. The flesh was seduced to lust, the eyes to long, and pride to covet. As the acorn contains the monarch of the forest, and the seed, the planks for the great mansions and mighty ships, so do these three things constitute "all that is in the world" and beyond them Satan has nothing to offer to man. Notice carefully that they emphasise the body, not the spirit; time, not eternity; the world, not God.

What is the practical lesson for us all? This: that our only hope when temptation assails us is to turn from it instantly and cleave to our God.   For the poet speaks the sober truth when he tells us that

> "Vice is a monster of such fearful mien,
> That to be hated needs but to be seen;
> Yet seen too oft, familiar with her face,
> We first endure, then pity, then embrace."

"Where," you may ask, "where was God when this tragedy was being enacted? Why did He not step in and prevent the awful calamity?" Let us recognise at once that we can easily get beyond our depth here. "The Bible gives no solution of the origin of evil, because that is merely a speculative question. Not to show us how it began but how to make an end of it is the object of the Bible. The origin of evil must remain where we find it, shrouded in impenetrable mystery, until we are constituted differently from what we are, and can see things in God's light." Meantime, let us hold fast to the assurance of the goodness, righteousness, and love of God as these are unveiled to us in Christ.   And let us recognise that

> "The ills we see,
> The mysteries of suffering deep and long,
> The dark enigmas of permitted wrong
> Have all one key;
> This strange sad world is but our Father's school,
> All chance and change His love doth grandly over-rule."

One of the philosophers has truthfully said that the present and the future may be set forth by a point of interrogation and a point of exclamation with a thin line between them. Thus:

!
—
?

Below, the questions of time; above, the hallelujahs of eternity. Here, dim vision and partial knowledge: there, face to face and knowing as we are known (1 Cor. 13. 12.).

3. THE INVESTIGATION (VERSES 9-13)

The immediate consequences of the Fall were two-fold: a sense of shame (verse 7) and a dread of judgment (verse 10). There was the consciousness of nakedness, and of the loss of rectitude. No longer at home in the presence of God—erect, confident, true—they seek to hide themselves in the garden of the Lord, from the Lord of the garden.

The investigation opens by God Himself Who puts a question to each of them. To Adam He says: "Where art thou?" (verse 9), and to Eve: "What is this that thou hast done?" (verse 13). These questions are at once searching, compelling, revealing; from them there is no escape.

"Where art thou?" That is the saddest question in all history. It is the enquiry of divine justice which cannot overlook sin; of divine sorrow which grieves over the sinner; of divine love which offers redemption from sin. (Compare this, the first question asked by God in the Old Testament, with Matthew 2. 2—"where is He?"—which is the first question asked by man in the New Testament. In the one you have God seeking man; in the other you have man seeking God.)

"I was afraid." This is the first time that the word "afraid" occurs in the biblical story of man. Dr. Parker has pointed out how instructive it is to mark the entrance of great words into human speech. Sin has a dictionary of its own. Fear, sorrow, pain, shame, grief, death—so runs the dreadful catalogue. With Adam, fear took the place of confidence, and terror that of trust.

> "Thus oft it haps that when within,
> They shrink at sense of secret sin,
> A feather daunts the brave;
> A fool's wild speech confounds the wise,
> And proudest princes veil their eyes
> Before the meanest slave."

In the answers to these questions given by the guilty pair we have another consequence of the Fall, namely, the attempt to escape responsibility for wrong-doing.

Adam admits his guilt but does not confess it: indeed he indirectly blames God Himself for it: "The woman whom Thou gavest to be with me, she gave me of the tree and I did eat" (verse 12). Eve blames the serpent (verse 13). What a degrading thing is sin. It destroys all honesty and candour, and, like conscience, makes cowards of us all.

These then are the moral effects of the Fall—shame, fear, flight, evasion, meanness, concealment.

CHAPTER EIGHT

THE FALL AND ITS CONSEQUENCES (2)

WE pass now to examine the penal consequences of sin, in doing which we shall find a wondrous mingling of mercy and judgment. First of all the guilty ones are

4. SENTENCED (VERSES 4-10)

By allowing the man and the woman to state their case the evil was traced to its source. "Actually and principally Satan was responsible for the Fall, and God charged him with it (Genesis 3. 14; 2 Corinthians 11. 3); instrumentally and subjectively Eve was responsible, and God charged her with it (Genesis 3. 13; 1 Timothy 2. 14); morally and representatively Adam was accountable and God charged him with it (Genesis 3. 17; Romans 5. 12)." Punishment, as we shall see, was to be not vindictive but disciplinary; not the result of excitement, but the expression of divine law. And it is interesting to notice that whereas in the enquiry God dealt first with the man, then the woman, and then the serpent, when He pronounces sentence on each He does so in the reverse order.

(1) The serpent—Satan's tool—is cursed (verse 14) and becomes God's illustration in nature of the effects of sin. From being a model of grace and excellence in form it has become the emblem of all that is disgusting and low, branded with infamy and avoided with horror.

(2) The woman (verse 16). Carefully observe that while the serpent and the earth were cursed (verses 14 and 17) God did not curse the man or the woman. Nevertheless, they both have to suffer; and the woman suffers as wife and mother. Motherhood—the most sacred function committed to her—is linked and crowned with sorrow (verse 16). The entrance of sin into the world

necessitated a headship which was vested in Adam (verse 16); but very beautifully is it said later on that "a virtuous woman is a crown to her husband" (Proverbs 12. 4).

(3) The man (verses 17-19). The lot that falls to man is threefold:

(a) SORROW (verse 17). Sorrow as the consequence of sin is branded on the forehead of humanity by the hand of a righteous God, and that so deeply that no devices of man can possibly remove its mark. "It is the belief of the heathen; it is the creed of the Christian; it is the record of the historian; it is the maxim of the philosopher; it is the song of the poet." The man that is a stranger to sorrow has never yet been born (Job 5. 7).

(b) TOIL (verse 19). That a change came upon the physical world consequent on man's sin is clearly taught both in the Old and New Testaments (Genesis 3. 17; Romans 8. 20-22 R.V.); and Adam is told that the light and pleasant occupation of Eden is to be exchanged for burdensome and unending labour. Once the soil yielded spontaneous abundance; now it yields to man only the bare necessities of life as he toils in sweat of face and with anxiety of heart. Although the text has only in view the simple life of the husbandman, the principle laid down extends to universal man. "Thorns also and thistles shall it bring forth to thee" until the time so graphically described by the seer when "instead of the thorn shall come up the fir tree, and instead of the brier, the myrtle tree" (Isaiah 55. 13). Meantime, "it is better to battle with a reluctant earth than to live without toil."

(c) DEATH. "Dust thou art and unto dust shalt thou return" (verse 19). These words remind us of the frailty of our frame, and declare the certainty of its dissolution. Abraham (Genesis 18. 27), Job (Job

10. 9), David (Psalm 103. 14), and Solomon (Ecclesiastes 3. 20), were all conscious of the first fact; the New Testament in clear and unambiguous words declares the truth about the second (Romans 5. 12; Hebrews 9. 27). "It is appointed unto men once to die." The heart of each member of the human race is, to use Longfellow's striking simile, like a muffled drum beating a funeral march to the grave. Sin and death are as closely linked together as are cause and effect.

The Dawn of Promise (Verse 15)

The gloom was, however, not wholly unrelieved; for in verse 15 the lamp of prophecy is lit, revealing the promise and the method of man's redemption. The seed of the woman—true but sinless Man—was to be the Conqueror of man's conqueror; but the victory was to be won through suffering. In the very heart of the curse, therefore, we have the germ of redemption.

The Dawn of Faith (Verse 20)

If verse 15 is the dawn of promise, verse 20 is the dawn of faith. Adam took up once more his divinely conferred prerogative of naming, and called his wife Eve—that is life, or life giver. Although sentence of death had been pronounced, his faith laid hold of the promise that through the seed of the woman life should come.

But our first parents were not only sentenced; they were also

5. CLOTHED (VERSE 21)

Since up to this point animal food had not been permitted to man, the brief incidental mention of the fact that the guilty pair were clothed with "coats of skin" is full of spiritual significance. These divinely provided coverings, which took the place of the man-made aprons, necessitated the shedding of blood. Before they could be procured, the animals to which they belonged had to be slain; and hence we have here the foreshadowing of a sacrifice which should finally atone for sin and provide for man a robe of righteousness. Indeed the little verse is a suggestion in miniature of the whole plan of redemption through the shed blood of a substitutionary victim. "Christ the Lamb of God gave up His life in order to provide a robe of righteousness for guilty man" (Isaiah 64. 6 and 61. 10; Romans 3. 21-22; 2 Corinthians 5. 21).

It should be carefully noted that while this seamless robe is unto all—that is, within reach of all; it is only upon all them that believe (Romans 3. 22). Genesis 3. 21 shows how it was procured; Genesis 15. 6 shows how it is received.

Finally the primeval pair were

6. BANISHED (VERSES 22-24)

As fallen, man is not allowed to eat of the tree of life for that would entail upon him endless wretchedness in this world. The tree of life can be tasted only in resurrection. "So He drove out the man."

> "The fatal fall, the sin, the shame,
> The doom, the death, the sword aflame:
> The crime, the curse, the tear-filled eyes,
> And earth no more is paradise."

Banished from the earthly paradise, however, it is possible for us now by grace divine to enter the heavenly one; and the remainder of God's book explains how this comes about.

And now, to quote the words of Pember, "the garden of Eden disappears from view, and is scarcely ever mentioned again until we come to the last of the books of revelation. But in the Apocalypse it rises before us once more in all its pristine beauty and we see the sons of Adam walking on the banks of the crystal stream, and no longer excluded from the tree of life."

CHAPTER NINE

THE SEVEN OUTSTANDING REVELATIONS OF GENESIS 1-3

WE have dealt somewhat in detail with the first three chapters of Genesis because of their supreme importance; and before passing on to the remaining portion of the book, we propose briefly to recapitulate, and where necessary, to expand what has been before us. We shall do this most effectively, perhaps, by pointing out the seven outstanding revelations of these chapters; revelations which begin with an unveiling of the personality of God, and end by showing us how we may be fitted to dwell in His presence.

1. THE PERSONALITY OF GOD

The fact of a Creator is the fundamental teaching of Genesis 1. "In the first verse of Genesis in words of supernatural grandeur, we have a revelation of God as the first Cause, the Creator of the universe, the world, and man. The glorious Being of God comes forth without explanation, and without apology. It is a revelation of the one, personal, living God." That revelation becomes deeper and fuller as the books of Scripture come to be written, until finally it culminates in Christ (John 1. 18; 14. 9); but confining ourselves to the book which we are studying we find that chapter 1 unveils His power (Romans 1. 20); chapter 2, His wisdom (Psalm 139. 14); chapters 3 and 4, His justice and grace; chapters 5 to 9, His holiness; chapters 10 and 11, His sovereignty (Daniel 4. 35); chapters 12 to 25, His faithfulness; chapters 26 to 36, His patience (Psalm 146. 5); and chapters 37 to 50, His providence (see Genesis 45. 1-9).

It should be carefully noted that the revelation of God

is unargued truth. God, Who is the Author of the Bible, no more argues His own existence than does a human author begin his book by proving that he himself actually lives. There is only one man who says there is no God: Scripture calls him the fool; and even he says it, not in his head, but in his heart. The wish is father to the thought.

2. THE CREATION OF THE UNIVERSE

Creation—the universe—is a revelation of God's power and assures us that He lives (Romans 1. 20); the Scriptures —His Word—are a revelation of His heart and assure us that He loves (John 3. 16). Psalm 19. 1-6 celebrates the first of these; verses 7-11 extol the second.

After the statement of Genesis 1. 1, the story of the Bible is confined to earth and its inhabitants; and careful examination of the remaining verses of that chapter will give us an explanation of the facts and forces in the midst of which we find ourselves to-day. Genesis 1 tells us how the world was made; Genesis 3, how it was lost; John 1 tells us how it was redeemed (verse 29); and Isaiah 11 how it will be renewed (see also Romans 8. 19-23 R.V.).

3. THE ORIGIN AND UNITY OF THE HUMAN RACE

It is very clearly stated both in the Old and New Testaments that all human beings have the unity of a common descent. This is definitely affirmed by the Lord Jesus (Matthew 19. 4) and by the Apostle Paul (Romans 5. 12; 1 Corinthians 15). We shall see when we come to Genesis 10 and 11 that the human race was divided into nations; but these divisions, clearly recognised in Scripture and by secular historians, are divisions of the human family. "God that made the world and all things therein . . . hath made of one blood all nations of men to dwell on all the face of the earth, and hath determined the times before appointed, and the bounds of their habitation" (Acts 17. 24-26).

4. How Sin Entered the World

If you will compare the first four words of Genesis
with the last four, you will find a contrast which is at
once startling and appalling. "In the beginning God"—
"A coffin in Egypt." The living God—a dead man.
Between these two expressions lies the catastrophe recorded in chapter 3—a catastrophe the effects of which
shall go on devastating the earth till the last syllable of
recorded time. It is the fall of man and the entrance of
sin (Romans 5. 12). Genesis 3 shows us how sin affects
the individual; chapter 4, how it affects the family; and
and chapters 5 and 6, how it affects the race.

5. Man's Unrelenting Enemy

The following poem describes a doctrine which finds
well-nigh universal acceptance to-day—the doctrine of
"no devil"; but it also raises some very pertinent questions which are suggested by the proclamation of that
doctrine.

THE DEVIL

"Men don't believe in a devil now as their fathers used to
do;
They forced the door of the broadest creed to let his
majesty through.
There isn't a print of his cloven foot, or a fiery dart
from his bow,
To be found in earth or air to-day, for the world has
voted so.

But who is it mixes the fatal draught that palsies heart
and brain,
And loads the bier of each passing year with a hundred
thousand slain?
Who blights the bloom of the land to-day with the
fiery breath of hell,
If the devil isn't and never was? Won't somebody rise
and tell?

Who dogs the steps of a toiling saint, and digs the pit
for his feet?
Who sows the tares in the field of time wherever God
sows His wheat?
The devil is voted not to be, and, of course the thing
is true;
But who is doing the kind of work the devil alone should
do?

We are told he does not go around like a roaring lion
now;
But whom shall we hold responsible for the everlasting
row
To be heard in home, in church and state, to the earth's
remotest bound,
If the devil by a unanimous vote is nowhere to be
found?

Won't somebody step to the front forthwith and make
their bow and show
How the frauds and crimes of a single day spring up?
We want to know.
The devil was fairly voted out, and, of course the devil's
gone;
But simple people would like to know who carries the
business on."

The Biblical records declare that there is in the universe
of God a being: powerful, malignant, cunning, who is in
rebellion against the Most High (Ezekiel 28); that he is
primarily responsible for the entrance of sin into our
world (Genesis 3); and that he is the bitter and relentless
foe of the human race (Job 1). "The Lord said unto
Satan: whence comest thou? Then Satan answered the
Lord and said: from going to and fro in the earth, and from
walking up and down in it" (Job 1. 7). These words
contain "the sob of a weird unrest."

His activity among the children of men is threefold: he
seeks to blind them (2 Cor. 4. 4); when that fails he
endeavours to beguile them (chapter 11. 3); if unsuccessful
in these ways he buffets them (chapter 12. 7). The two
methods by which he works, therefore, are deception and

violence—as an angel of light (2 Cor. 11. 13-14), and as a roaring lion (1 Peter 5. 8).

6. The Fountain Head of Prophecy

Genesis 3. 15 is a germinal prophecy; it contains in embryo all that was subsequently revealed. "I will put enmity between thee and the woman"—Eve is no longer on the side of her deceiver; "and between thy seed and her seed"—there is the beginning of the agelong conflict which is now rapidly coming to a head; "He (the pronoun is masculine) shall bruise thy head, and thou shalt bruise His heel"—these words tell us of the effects of the first and second comings of our Lord.

The coming One was to be of the human race (Genesis 3. 15); of the line of Abraham (Genesis 12. 3); of the tribe of Judah (Genesis 49. 10); and of the family of David (2 Samuel 7. 16). He would be born of a virgin (Isaiah 7. 14); and in Bethlehem of Judea (Micah 5. 2). For the fulfilment of all these things in the order in which I have mentioned them see:—Luke 19. 10; Hebrews 2. 16; Hebrews 7. 14; Matthew 21. 9; Matthew 1. 16; Matthew 2. 1-6.

7. The Method of Redemption

"Unto Adam also and to his wife did the Lord God make coats of skin, and clothed them" (Genesis 3. 21). Here we have the primal revelation of sacrifice. The fig leaves of their own providing were ineffectual and insufficient; the robe with which God clothed them, secured as it was by the shedding of blood, foreshadows the great truth of righteousness based upon sacrifice. "All our righteousnesses are as filthy rags"—there are the fig leaves; "He hath covered me with the robe of righteousness"—there is the provision of the seamless robe (Isaiah 64. 6; 61. 10). The wardrobe of a Christian is the righteousness of God; and to quote the saintly McCheyne,

"When we stand before Thy throne, clothed in beauty not our own,

Then Lord shall we fully know, not till then how much we owe."

CHAPTER TEN

ABEL—Genesis 4.

WE now pass to the remaining portion of the book of Genesis—chapter 4 to chapter 50—which is largely biographical. In it we shall find seven outstanding names, each of which stands for a distinctive truth. Taken together these names and the truths which they illustrate give us, from another point of view, what we found in the first chapter of Genesis, namely, a perfect picture of the development of the life divine in the soul of man. They are as follows:

	Name	Truth	Chapter
1.	Abel.	Acceptance.	4.
2.	Enoch.	Communion.	5.
3.	Noah.	Testimony.	6-10.
4.	Abraham.	Obedience.	11-25.
5.	Isaac.	Sonship.	21-27.
6.	Jacob.	Discipline.	27-36.
7.	Joseph.	Victory.	37-50.

You will observe that of all the men whose names appear in the book of Genesis, the above seven are the only ones mentioned in Hebrews 11—the roll call of Faith.

(1) ABEL: GENESIS 4
Outline of the Chapter

The first motherhood	Verse 1.
The first family	Verse 2.
The first worshippers	Verse 3-5.
The first murderer	Verse 6-8.
The first martyr	Verse 9-10.
The first civilization	Verse 16-22.

The matter of supreme importance to us in this chapter is brought before us in verses 3 to 5 which describe

The First Worshippers

In enquiring why it was that Abel's offering was accepted and Cain's rejected, there is something which we must carefully remember. From the moment that sin entered the world, man was separated from God by the distance of death (Genesis 2. 17). We have a clear hint of this in Genesis 3. 21. The coats of skin by which the guilty pair had been fitted to dwell in His presence necessitated the shedding of blood, the taking of life. Since the Fall, therefore, man can approach God only on the ground of death. Now these two young men would be carefully instructed by their parents regarding this solemn fact; but the sequal shows that, while Abel believed and bowed to the instruction, Cain ignored it altogether.

Abel's Offering: Verse 4

"Abel brought of the firstlings of his flock and of the fat thereof"; and linking that Scripture with Hebrews 11. 4, we learn that it was offered "by faith." Faith always presupposes a divine revelation to which it is the response; for faith cometh by hearing and hearing by the Word of God (Romans 10. 17). In this case the revelation was that of the method by which God could be approached. Abel recognised the fact of sin, the penalty of which is death; and when he came to his Creator he placed the shed blood of a substitutionary victim between himself and God, and seems to say: "Death is what I deserve and I confess it; but I come to Thee depending entirely on the merits of another." His sacrifice, in which atoning blood was shed, was therefore at once his confession of sin and his faith in the interposition of a substitute. It was the recognition by the man of faith in the twilight of the world's history that without the shedding of blood there is no remission (Hebrews 9. 22). And that in effect is what every believer in Christ is doing to-day. Abel's lamb prefigures the Lamb of God which taketh away the sin of the world; and when we approach our God relying on the merits of that sacrifice, we do so in the spirit of the well-known words:

> "Nothing in my hand I bring,
> Simply to Thy cross I cling,
> Could my zeal no langour know,
> Could my tears forever flow—
> These for sin could not atone,
> But Thy blood and Thine alone."

Cain's Offering: Verse 3

"Cain brought of the fruit of the ground an offering unto the Lord." That is to say, he offered that which sustains life, while God was demanding life itself. It has been pointed out that he neither denied the existence of God nor did he refuse to worship Him; that he recognised God as the Giver of every good and perfect gift, and brought an offering of the fruit of the ground as acknowledgment of His bounty. But he went no further than this. His was not the worship of a false God; it was false worship of the true God—that is, worship not preceded by salvation. Cain's religion was destitute of any sense of sin or need of atonement. He rejected God's way of access and God rejected him.

These two men are representative men; and two New Testament Scriptures bring before us the respective systems for which they stand. One is called "the way of Cain" (Jude 11); the other, "the new and living way" (Hebrews 10. 19-20). Two altars have been erected in the world, and at one or the other of these all men are worshipping. The altar of Cain is piled high with richest fruit, choicest grain, and the most delicately perfumed flowers—the modern equivalents of these being an ornate ritual, enchanting music, imposing and elaborate ceremonies. But there is no hint of the shedding of blood there; and without the shedding of blood there is no remission.

The other is the altar of Abel on which rests the slain lamb. Let us with unfaltering lips proclaim the great and blessed truth which it foreshadows. "Without the atonement" says good Bishop Ryle, "the gospel is like a fair building without a foundation, like an arch without a key-stone, like a solar system without a sun." Without it, we may truthfully add, the historical portion of the Bible becomes meaningless, the doctrinal structures become valueless, the ethical teaching becomes powerless.

"Blest Lamb of God, Thy precious blood shall never
　　lose its power
Till every ransomed saint of God be saved to sin
　　no more."

To sum up: Abel's altar speaks of repentance, faith, the shedding of blood, and the spotless lamb. Cain's speaks of pride, self-will, unbelief, and self-righteousness.

The first Martyr

Genesis 3. 15 clearly indicates that there were to be two seeds in deadly antagonism to each other: the seed of the woman, and the seed of the serpent; and in 1 John 3. 12 it is distinctly stated that Cain was of the seed of the serpent. He was a murderer (Genesis 4. 8) and a liar (verse 9)—precisely the two things which are true of the devil himself (John 8. 44). And so we learn the sad truth that sin which ruined the first man, prompted the second man to slay the third man. Abel was the first martyr to the truth of acceptance (Matthew 23. 35), just as Stephen was the first martyr to the truth of resurrection (Acts 7. 56-60).

The first Civilization

Going out from the presence of the Lord (verse 16), Cain and his descendants sought to reproduce Eden artificially, and to make themselves as comfortable as possible on a blighted and blasted earth. They founded a city (verse 17) in which appeared every element of material civilization—agriculture (verse 20); music (verse 21); manufactures (verse 22); while verses 23-24 give us the first recorded specimen of primeval poetry. It should be noted that Jubal was the discoverer of what to this day are regarded as the only two real methods of producing music—the stringed instrument—the harp; and the wind instrument—the organ (verse 21).

But while it was progress, it was progress away from God. Self-contained and self-centred they spent their days as though God never existed, and lived and died without Him.

CHAPTER ELEVEN

ENOCH—Genesis 5

IF the 4th chapter of Genesis gives us the record of the Cainites who lived their lives in independence of God, the 5th chapter tells the story of the Sethites who called upon His name and sought the knowledge of His ways.

The seventh in the line of Cain was Lamech—a man who was at once a murderer, a polygamist, and a worshipper of the god of force (4. 23). The seventh in the line of Seth was Enoch—a man of whom it is written that he walked with God; who had this testimony, that he pleased God; and of whom, finally, it is declared that he was translated to heaven by God. It is to this man's biography—which tells of a life of hallowed and unbroken communion with God—that I desire now to turn.

One of the lies with which Satan deceived our first mother was: "Ye shall not surely die"; but the phrase "and he died" which we find eight times in this chapter is a complete vindication of the solemn warning of God. For death is a

> "Judgment of God no mortal may repeal,
> Crushing our fairest in its ruthlessness,
> Mocking our love-sighs in its brutalness,
> Tearing our hearts with wounds that none can heal."

The patriarchal funeral bell tolls for the sixth time; but when we come to Enoch we find something extremely unusual. Instead of saying of him, as he says of the others, that Enoch merely lived so many years and then died, the writer says that "Enoch walked with God: and he was not; for God took him" (verse 24).

Four things are said of him:

(1) HE WALKED WITH GOD (GENESIS 5. 24)

That implies that at some point in his career he came into agreement with God; for how can two walk together except they are agreed? (Amos 3. 3). The record does not definitely state when that point was reached, but the language of verse 22 suggests that it was on the occasion of the birth of his little son.

God has now made very clear where a holy walk begins, and where for the first time He can meet with sinful men. That point is the anti-typical mercy-seat, the place of sacrifice—Calvary. "There will I meet with thee" (Exodus 25. 22). The extreme beauty of that statement is seen when it is read in connection with Romans 3. 24-26 and when it is remembered that the word translated "propitiation" in verse 25 is literally "mercy-seat".

Consequent on that agreement, and as uninterruptedly he walked with God, there were three things which Enoch would experience in ever-increasing degree, namely, heavenly companionship, abounding joy and perfect rest. We may do the same to-day (see Hebrews 13. 5; Psalm 16. 11; Exodus 33. 14).

> "To walk with God! Oh, fellowship Divine—
> Man's highest state on earth—Lord be it mine!
> With Thee may I a close communion hold,
> To Thee the deep recesses of my heart unfold—
> Yes, tell Thee all; each dreary care and grief
> Into Thy bosom pour, till there I find relief.
> Oh, let me walk with Thee, Thou Mighty One!
> Lean on Thine arm, and trust Thy love alone.
> With Thee hold converse sweet where'er I go,
> Thy smile of love my highest bliss below."

(2) HE WITNESSED FOR GOD (JUDE 14-15)

The appearance of the prophet always implies a previous departure on the part of the people from God; and the substance of Enoch's prophecy clearly indicates that so it was with his contemporaries. His message was a message of judgment; and his words would be thunder because his life was lightning. He became a kind of incarnate conscience to the people among whom he lived.

(3) HE WAS WELL-PLEASING TO GOD (HEBREWS 11. 5)

If it were not clearly revealed to us in His Word we should never have conceived the thought that it is possible for mortal man, amid the toil and the sorrow and the heartache incidental to life on this earth, to give pleasure to the eternal God. The Scriptures, however, not only reveal that this is possible but clearly indicate some of the methods by which it may be done (Colossians 1. 9-10; 1 Thessalonians 4. 1).

To begin with it should be noted that there are two classes who cannot please God, namely those who are destitute of faith (Hebrews 11. 6) and those who are in the flesh (Romans 8. 8). That is another way of saying that the faith which is illustrated in Abel must precede that which is illustrated in Enoch; that we must be accepted by God before we can be acceptable to God.

Given that indispensable prerequisite, however, we learn (1) that the yielding to Him of our bodies a living sacrifice (Romans 12. 1); (2) that doing good to men and women everywhere (Hebrews 13. 16; Galatians 6. 10); (3) that the giving of material help to the servants of God (Philippians 4. 18); and (4) that the fruit of our lips giving thanks to His name (Hebrews 13. 15; 1 Thessalonians 5. 18) are things, all of which are acceptable or well-pleasing to God.

A woman who wears the ornament of a meek and quiet spirit wears that which in the sight of God is of great price (1 Peter 3. 1-4); a man who, consciously in the right, has to suffer as if he were in the wrong, who does so patiently and uncomplainingly, gives pleasure to God (1 Peter 2. 19-20); and even the little children may avail themselves of this high privilege; for the word to them is: "Children, obey your parents in all things: for this is well-pleasing unto the Lord" (Colossians 3. 20).

As usual, we find that God's commands are His enablings. He waits to work in us that which is well-pleasing in His sight (Hebrews 13. 21); and to enable us to will and to do of His good pleasure (Philippians 2. 11-13). Some are willing but are not able; others are able but are not willing; but He imparts both the desire and the ability.

Our Master is our model: He did always those things that pleased God (John 8. 29); and with Him before us, we shall do well to adopt as our own that which formed the apostle's life-long endeavour: "We make it our aim," he says, "that whether present or absent, we may be well-pleasing to Him" (2 Cor. 5. 9 R.V.).

(4) HE WAS TRANSLATED BY GOD (HEBREWS 11. 5)

"He changed his place but not his company."

The Genesis record merely says that "he was not, for God took him," but the law of recurrence comes to our aid here and shows us that these words do not mean that he died, but that he did not see death; that he left the world, not by the dark tunnel of death, but by the golden bridge of translation; that he vanished into the heavenly land like the setting of

> "The morning star which goes
> Not down behind the darkened west, nor hides
> Obscured amid the tempests of the sky,
> But melts away into the light of heaven."

"God took him—it is the assertion of a sovereign right; it is an illustration of divine regard; it is an assurance of eternal blessedness; it is a pledge that all like him will be associated."

If Abel's lamb points back to the cross of our Lord, Enoch's translation points us on to the coming of the Lord. The one speaks to us of the foundation upon which we rest; and the other, of the hope for which we wait.

"Will this year bring the coming of the Lord?
        I cannot say.
But I will live and move and have my being
        In Him from day to day.
I will walk softly through the shadows listening
        For His dear voice,
Who tells me He is coming—coming quickly—
        And therefore I rejoice."

CHAPTER TWELVE

NOAH—Genesis 6-8.

ABEL, Enoch and Noah follow each other not only historically but also in the order of spiritual experience. It is only the man who has been accepted by God as was Abel, that can walk with God as did Enoch; and it is only the man who walks with God as did Enoch, that can give powerful testimony for God as did Noah.

We shall look (1) at what is said about Noah—the man; (2) at the event which formed the central thing in his life; and (3) at what happened after he stood on the renewed earth.

Noah—the Man

(a)	The favour which he found	Gen. 6.8.
(b)	The character which he bore	Gen. 6.9.
(c)	The fellowship which he enjoyed	Gen. 6.9.
(d)	The obedience which he rendered	Gen. 6.22.
(e)	The testimony which he gave	Heb. 11.7.
(f)	The invitation which he received	Gen. 7.1.
(g)	The kindness which he experienced	Gen. 8.1.
(h)	The altar which he erected	Gen. 8.20.
(i)	The covenant which he inherited	Gen. 9.11.
(j)	The sin which he committed	Gen. 9.21.

The Ark and the Flood

As space forbids adducing the scientific and archæological evidence of the truthfulness of the narrative before us, we shall merely quote Old and New Testament Scriptures to show that the Flood was an historical event (Job 22. 15, 16; Isaiah 54. 9; Matthew 24. 37-39; 1 Peter 3. 20); and that Noah was an historical person (Ezekiel 14. 14; 2 Peter 2. 5-6).

The picture drawn by the historian in the sixth chapter

of Genesis is one of the most appalling description. Two words sum up the conditions which obtained: corruption and violence (verse 11). These are the two great forms of human wickedness—the inward and the outward; and they are as related to each other as are cause and effect.

God waited long and patiently, but at length the hour of judgment arrived. Here as always, however, there is a wondrous mingling of mercy and judgment; for just as on the night of the passover when God announced the doom of the guilty land He also gave instructions about the sheltering blood: so when informing Noah of the impending flood He instructed him also about the sheltering ark.

The chapter is in three sections:

(1) *The Verdict which God Pronounced* (*verses* 1-6)

"God saw that the wickedness of man was great in the earth, and that every imagination of the thoughts of his heart was only evil continually" (verse 5); and because of these things He further said: "The end of all flesh is come before me" (verse 13). These matters are of the deepest interest to us; for our Lord assures us that, as it was in the days which were before the Flood, so will it be in the days preceding the coming of the Son of Man (Matthew 24. 37-39).

(2) *The Judgment which God Proclaimed* (*verses* 7-13)

The announcement of the deluge was made in language of the most solemn description. The section begins and ends with the words: "I will destroy." Lawlessness, corruption, and violence had become universal, and the judgment was to be co-extensive with the evil. Here again we are reminded of the words of our Lord (Luke 17. 26, 27).

(3) *The Remedy which God Provided (verses 14-22)*

In the midst of the general apostasy however, one man stood loyal; and to him God reveals His purposes and discloses His mind. "Noah found grace in the eyes of the Lord" (Gen. 6. 8); and "being warned of God of things not seen as yet, he moved with fear and prepared an ark to the saving of his house, by which he condemned the world, and became heir of the righteousness which is by faith" (Hebrews 11. 7). Details of the ark are given in the section now before us; and Noah carried out his instructions to the letter (verse 22).

The word translated "warned" in Hebrews 11. 7 means "to be divinely instructed"; and bearing that in mind we have in this verse:

(a) The basis of faith—he was instructed by God.

(b) The sphere of faith—it lives among things not seen as yet.

(c) The attitude of faith—he moved with fear.

(d) The obedience of faith—he prepared an ark.

(e) The efficacy of faith—it saved his house.

(f) The testimony of faith—in building the ark he condemned the world.

(g) The reward of faith—he became heir of the righteousness which is by faith.

Carefully note that although he was a preacher of righteousness (2 Peter 2. 5) and gave powerful testimony for God, his preaching consisted not so much in what he said, as in what he did. His faith, his conduct, and his work, were all in perfect harmony. The trouble with many of us is that our conduct is so out of harmony with our testimony that the latter is deprived of all its power. Is it not Emerson who has said: "What you are, speaks so loudly that I cannot hear what you say"?

Outline of Genesis 7 and 8

In these two chapters we have the story of Noah's:

(1) Entrance to the Ark   Chapter 7. 1-16.

(2) Safety in the Ark   Chapter 7. 16—8. 14.

(3) Exit from the Ark   Chapter 8. 15—22.

(1) *Entrance.* The invitation to enter the ark was given to Noah seven days before the rain descended; and one can understand how God's servant would be ridiculed by his contemporaries. Someone has said that if there were daily newspapers in those days, the following note would have appeared on the sixth day before the deluge: "Yesterday afternoon the madness of our esteemed friend Noah, who for 120 years has been preparing for a rainy day, took a new turn. Together with his family and representatives of the animal creation he moved inside the ark which he has been constructing; and we counsel all our readers who want a bit of fun to go and see the vessel in which he sits self-imprisoned." "They did not realize any danger till the deluge came and swept them all away" (Matthew 24. 35-39 Weymouth).

(2) *Preservation.* The language which was used when Noah was invited to enter the ark and commanded to leave it, implies that in a very real sense God was with him during his stay there. For the invitation reads: "Come thou . . . into the ark"—God was there before him (Genesis 7. 1); and after the judgment was over the command was: "Go forth out of the ark"—God was the last to leave it (chapter 8. 16). "His presence is salvation."

(3) *Exit.* It is stated that God remembered Noah (chapter 8. 1); but in this section we learn that Noah remembered God: he builded an altar unto the Lord (chapter 8. 20). By so doing he "testified at once to his gratitude to God for deliverance, to his need of sacrifice in approaching God, and to the consecration of his life to

the service of God as symbolised by the burnt-offering."

And now before passing from this theme we shall look at some of the gospel lessons which we learn from the ark.

(a) *It was an expression of God's love* (*Chapter* 6. 14)

Judgment was impending and the doom of the world announced; but a refuge was provided: Noah need not perish (John 3. 16).

(b) *It bore the storm* (*chapter* 7. 11-12)

It thus foreshadowed what Isaiah more specifically announced: "a man shall be as an hiding place from the wind, and a covert from the tempest" (Isaiah 32. 2).

> "The tempest's awful voice was heard,
> O Christ, it broke on Thee;
> Thy open bosom was my ward,
> It braved the storm for me;
> Thy form was scarred, Thy vision marred,
> Now cloudless peace for me."

(c) *It was a place of safety* (*chapter* 6. 14)

The word translated "pitch" in Genesis 6. 14 is the same word that is translated "atonement" in Leviticus 17. 11. Those in the ark are thus a picture of those "in Christ". "It is atonement that keeps out the waters of judgment and makes the believer's position safe and blessed." Other refuge have I none.

(d) *It had only one door of entrance* (*chapter* 6. 16)

Immediately after Noah entered the ark we read that the Lord shut him in (chapter 7. 16). He had entered by divine invitation; he was kept by divine power. Compare this with John 10. 9 and 10. 27-28.

> "Let me no more my comfort draw
> From my frail hold on Thee;
> In this alone rejoice with awe—
> Thy mighty grasp of me."

(e) *It had only one window* (*chapter* 6. 16)

The door was in the side of the ark; the window was above. The former—of which God had charge—speaks of salvation; the latter—of which Noah had charge—speaks of communion. Noah had simply to count on the faithfulness of God and keep "looking up".

(f) *It rested on resurrection ground* (*chapter* 8. 4)

In Exodus 12. 2 we learn that, consequent on the redemption which was effected for Israel on the night of the passover, the seventh month was changed into the first month. The paschal lamb was to be taken on the tenth day of that month, and slain on the fourteenth day. Three days thereafter would thus bring us to what was originally the seventeenth day of the seventh month.

Our Lord—the true passover Lamb—was crucified on the fourteenth day of the month and rose again the third day afterwards—exactly the day on which the ark rested on one of the mountains of Ararat.

(g) *The invitation to enter was personal and urgent* (*chapter* 7. 1)

"Come thou"; "Come now" (2 Corinthians 6. 2).

After Noah's emergence from the ark we hear no more about it. Lest it should become an object of worship as did the brazen serpent (2 Kings 18. 4), it was, in all probability, destroyed. Noah worshipped, not the ark, but the God of the ark; just as we worship, not the cross, but Him Who hung upon it.

"Blest cross, blessed sepulchre, blest rather be
    The Man Who there was put to shame for me."

"Superstition makes everything of God's ordinance; infidelity makes nothing of it; faith uses it according to divine appointment."

Chapter Thirteen

NATIONS : BABEL

GENESIS chapter nine is in three sections:

(1) The Establishment of Human Government
Verses 1-7

From these verses we learn (a) that the lower orders are henceforth to be governed by fear and dread instead of by kindness and love (verses 1-2); (b) that animal food is now permitted to man, probably in mitigation of the curse (verses 3-4); and (c) that man himself is put under human as well as divine laws (verses 5-6).

In connection with the last of these—the government of man by man—the New Testament instructs us to obey the powers that be (Romans 13. 1-6) save only when such obedience would hinder us from carrying out the will of God (Acts 5. 29).

(2) The Covenant with Noah and its Token
Verses 8-17

As he stepped on to the new earth one of Noah's most pressing needs was the assurance that there would be no repetition of the awful calamity that had befallen the world; and the covenant now made with him by God gave him that (verses 9-11), and the further assurance that the regular procession of the seasons would continue (chapter 8. 22).

Of this covenant the bow in the cloud is the token or sign (verse 13). Here for the first time Nature becomes a symbol of deep spiritual significance. Later on "the stars of heaven and the sand by the seashore become to Abraham as a family register"; and if, as Parker says, we cultivate the spirit of moral interpretation, the birds of the air will remind us of our Father's tenderness, and the lilies of the field, of His care.

The rainbow is the child of the storm and sunshine; it is "the smiling offspring of the weeping storm." Three things are necessary to produce it—cloud, rain, and sun. "The cloud is needed as the canvas on which the bow of beauty shall be painted. The sun is needed to give the light—the colours of which the painting is composed. The drops of falling rain are needed by which the colours are applied—the medium required to decompose the rays of light and spread out their varying hues in blended loveliness."

There may be a cloud without a rainbow; but there cannot be a rainbow without a cloud. Its appearance tells us that however dark the cloud may be, the sun is shining still. And so it is with the dark and tragic things in our lives, of which the clouds are the symbol. The cloud of guilt is arched with the bow of pardon, and the cloud of mystery with the bow of providence; the cloud of sorrow is illumined with the bow of comfort, and the dark cloud of death with the radiant bow of hope.

"Through gloom and shadow look we on beyond the years;
The soul would have no rainbow had the eyes no tears."

As the rainbow is really a prismatic ring we shall, so long as we are on earth, see only a portion of it. Airmen have seen the full circle. Bye and bye when we ascend to the heavenly land we shall see the whole rainbow round about the throne (Revelation 4. 3). Now we know in part but then shall we know even as also we are known. Meantime,

"Be Thou the rainbow in the storms of life,
The evening beam that smiles the clouds away,
And tints to-morrow with prophetic ray."

(3) The Sin and Death of Noah. Verses 18-29

These verses illustrate the familiar saying that the best of men are but men at the best. Although Noah passed through thrilling experiences both of mercy and of judgment; although he was an heir of the righteousness which is by faith, and an honoured servant of God; and although he stood firm as a rock in testimony for God during times of adversity—yet when times of prosperity came, he tampered unduly with the wine-cup and brought a stain upon his otherwise blameless name. The lesson for us all is 1 Corinthians 10. 12: "Let him that thinketh he standeth take heed lest he fall".

The beginning of the Nations

If Genesis 3. 15 is the germ of prophecy, Genesis 9. 18 to 10. 32 is the germ of history. After a reaffirmation of the unity of the human race (Genesis 9. 19) we have "that miracle of ethnological prophecy by Noah in Genesis 9. 26-27, in which we have foretold in a sublime epitome the three great divisions of the human race, and their ultimate historical destinies. The three great divisions, Hamitic, Shemitic, and Japhetic, are the three ethnic groups into which modern science has divided the human race. The facts of history have fulfilled what was foretold in Genesis four thousand years ago. The Hamitic nations, including the Chaldean, Babylonic, and Egyptian, have been degraded, profane, and sensual. The Shemitic have been the religious with the line of the coming Messiah. The Japhetic have been the enlarging, and the dominant races, including all the great world monarchies, both of ancient and modern times: the Grecian, Roman, Gothic, Celtic, Teutonic, British and American, and by recent investigation and discovery, the races of India, China, and Japan. Thus Ham lost all empires centuries ago; Shem and his race acquired it ethically and spiritually through the prophet, priest, and king, the Messiah; while Japheth, in world-embracing and imperial supremacy, has stood for industrial, commercial, and political dominion."

It should, however, be carefully noted that, although in the providence of God the descendants of Ham were doomed to earthly inferiority, the Shemites blessed with spiritual privileges, and the Japhethites with supremacy and dominion, "grace overrides these distinctions and selects from all three branches of the human family those who will ultimately be one in a brighter and better world." Thus Acts 8 records the conversion of the Ethiopian Treasurer—a descendant of Ham; Acts 9 tells the story of the conversion of Saul of Tarsus—a descendant of Shem; and Acts 10, that of Cornelius—a descendant of Japheth.

All ethnological and philological investigation confirms the division of mankind into three primary groups from which the seventy nations of Genesis 10 descended. Brief and apparently uninteresting as are the verses of these chapters, it is a fact that they contain "the germ of every civilisation, the outline of every tragedy, the promise of final redemption and glory." Speaking broadly the Japhethites occupied the northern zone; the Shemites, the middle zone; and the Hamites, the southern zone.

There is a passage in Deuteronomy (chapter 32. 8) which throws great light on the divine purposes disclosed to us in Genesis 9, 10 and 11. "When the Most High divided to the nations their inheritance, when He separated the sons of Adam, He set the bounds of the people according to the number of the children of Israel." That is to say, that Israel was to be the centre of God's purposes in the redemption of the world, and that the nations of the earth were ranged around her in order to subserve that purpose. Let us who believe the Word of our God take the rich comfort which this fact is intended to yield. For in the midst of the turbulence and unrest which characterise the nations of the earth to-day, when men's hearts are failing them for fear because of the uncertainty of what is going to happen next, we ought never to forget that "He doeth according to His will in the army of heaven, and among the inhabitants of the earth, and none can stay His hand, or say unto Him: what doest Thou?" (Daniel 4. 34-35).

The Tower of Babel: Genesis 11

Genesis 10 and 11 should be read together. The former chapter declares the *fact* of the division of the nations and answers the question: How? (Genesis 10. 25; Deuteronomy 32. 8); the latter reveals the *cause* of the division and answers the question: Why? (chapter 11. 1-9).

There are words in the preceding section which clearly indicate that the purpose of God was that the sons of Noah should disperse over the face of the earth; but in Genesis 11 we come to an organised attempt to frustrate that purpose (verse 4). God intervened; and by confounding their speech, giving different tongues corresponding to the differences of race and family, providentially arranged that the descendants of Noah's three sons should go to the places assigned to them.

The following valuable note from the pen of Dr. Pierson describes the processes of the development, and the ultimate end both of Babel and its opposite. "In Babylon —the type of worldly civilisation—the law of association is mechanical centralization; the spirit is independence and rebellion against God's government; the aim is self-interest and self-glorification; the cult is materialism or idolatry; the method is autocracy and monopoly; the unifying bond is fear; the end is confusion.

In the new Jerusalem, the city of God, the law of association is brotherly fellowship; the spirit is loyal obedience to God; the aim is God's glory, and benevolence to all; the cult is spiritual worship of God alone; the method is social equality and co-operation; the unifying bond is love; and the end is perfect harmony."

Of the remaining portion of Genesis 11, verses 10 to 26 give the genealogy of Shem; and verses 27 to 32 that of Terah. Henceforth the line of the divine purpose runs along the last-named branch of the family of Shem.

CHAPTER FOURTEEN

ABRAHAM—OBEDIENCE

THOSE who have read the book of Genesis with care will have observed that from chapter 12 it ceases to be the history of humanity as a whole and becomes the story of a chosen man and his descendants. This man—Abram—was separated from the rest of the human race who were now rapidly sinking into idolatry; and he and the nation which sprang from him were blessed of God in order that ultimately they might be channels of blessing to universal man. "Henceforth in the Scripture record, humanity must be thought of as a vast stream from which God, in the call of Abraham and the creation of the nation of Israel, has but drawn off a slender rill through which He may at last purify the great river itself."

What stupendous results, therefore, hung upon Abraham's response to the call of God. Although an obscure and childless man living in an idolatrous land, grace divine selected him as the one through whom the blessing of Heaven should flow to earth's remotest bounds, and to the end of time.

Like him, we have turned to God from idols; and it may be that in your life God has not only personal, but also world-wide purposes; purposes that will make you His instrument for the enrichment of a sorrow-stricken world. Talk not of your insignificance and unworthiness, remember that

> "The smallest barque on life's tempestuous ocean
> Shall leave behind a track for evermore;
> The smallest wave of influence set in motion
> Extends and widens to the eternal shore."

When the name of any great biblical or historical personage is mentioned, we instinctively associate with it the trait or characteristic for which that person was famous. Thus, with Moses we associate the grace of meekness; with Samuel, integrity; with Elijah, courage; with Job, patience; with Daniel, faithfulness; with John, love; and with Paul, whole-hearted enthusiasm.

Two words are required to describe the outstanding traits of the life of Abraham: faith and obedience. He believed; and he obeyed. So marvellous was his faith and so absolute his obedience that, taking the three outstanding events of his life, we find that

(1) He believed when he knew not *where*. "By faith Abraham, when he was called to go out into a place which he should after receive for an inheritance, obeyed; and he went out, not knowing whither he went" (Hebrews 11. 8). He has been called the Columbus of faith, in that he went out with sealed orders and promises. He knew not the way which he travelled; but well did he know his Guide.

(2) He believed when he knew not *how*. He received the promise that his wife would have a son—an event which, because of Sarah's age, was a physiological impossibility; and we read that "being not weak in faith, he considered not his own body dead . . . neither yet the deadness of Sarah's womb; he staggered not at the promise of God through unbelief; but was strong in faith, giving glory to God; and being fully persuaded that, what He had promised, He was able also to perform" (Romans 4. 19-21; Hebrews 11. 11).

(3) He believed when he knew not *why*. Isaac was the sole link between him and the future blessing of the world of which God had spoken; and the command to sacrifice him seemed to contradict that promise. But unhesitatingly, "by faith Abraham, when he was tried, offered up Isaac: and he that had received the promises offered up his only begotten son, of whom it was said, that in Isaac shall thy seed be called: accounting that God was able to

raise him up even from the dead; from whence also he received him in a figure" (Hebrews 11. 17-19).

We have a saying to the effect that "confidence begets confidence," and that saying is strikingly illustrated in the life of Abraham. So intimate indeed became the fellowship which existed between him and his God, that on three separate occasions he is called the friend of God —2 Chronicles 20. 7; Isaiah 41. 8; James 2. 23. That friendship dignified and ennobled his life and made him a king among men. "In the combined grandeur and symmetry of his character he towers above a long line of illustrious descendants. He is characterised by the noblest qualities, without any of those great and aggravated faults by which the greatest virtues are frequently accompanied. David was not more regal in his bearing, and while like him he was kingly in all his movements, and was fitted by nature to be a ruler of men, he never indulged the lusts, nor was guilty of the sins which disgraced the shepherd king. Among all his sons he had no equal until He appeared Who infinitely surpassed him."

As the narrative proceeds, however, we shall find that we have before us, not a flawless angel, but a man of like passions with ourselves. "I am sorry," says Dr. Meredith, "I am sorry that these good old men were sometimes imperfect, but having sinned, I am glad their sins are recorded. How little hope there would be for us if all the Bible saints had been perfect."

But Abraham was not only the friend of God (James 2. 23) and the founder of the Jewish nation (Isaiah 51. 1-2); he was also the father of all that believe (Romans 4. 16; Galatians 3. 7). Each of us—true believers in the Lord Jesus Christ—possesses that mighty principle which linked him with Omnipotence; each of us may possess, on precisely the same terms, that sacred intimacy with the Most High which was the supreme privilege of his life. "Henceforth," says the Lord Jesus, "I call you not servants; for the servant knoweth not what his Lord doeth; but I have called you friends. Ye are My friends if ye do whatsoever I command you" (John 15. 14-15).

Abraham's life is described in Genesis 11. 27 to 25. 10; and I shall now give you a key-word for each of these chapters, and also point out the various traits of his character which the incidents recorded in them reveal.

Chapter	Keyword	Abraham's	Verses
12	Call	Obedience	1-5.
13	Lot	Unselfishness	8-9.
14	War	Courage	14-16.
15	Righteousness	Faith	6.
16	Hagar	Impatience	2.
17	Covenant	Incredulity	17.
18	Intercession	Hospitality	1-8.
19	Sodom	Ministry	29.
20	Abimelech	Failure	2.
21	Isaac	Joy	1-3.
22	Mt. Moriah	Trial	2.
23	Machpelah	Sorrow	2.
24	Rebekah	Wisdom	3-7.
25	Death	End	8.

Dates in Abraham's Life

It will help to a clearer understanding of the relation to each other of the various events in the life of Abraham if it is remembered that:

(1) Abraham was 75 years old when he entered Canaan (Genesis 12. 4).

(2) Ishmael was born 11 years after Abraham entered Canaan (Genesis 16. 16).

(3) Isaac was born 14 years after Ishmael (Genesis 21. 5).

(4) Abraham lived for 75 years after Isaac was born (Genesis 25. 7).

CHAPTER FIFTEEN

ABRAHAM (2)

Theophanies or Manifestations of God

IN the fourteen chapters which describe the life of Abraham there are eight recorded manifestations or appearances of God to him; manifestations, from each of which Abraham enters into richer blessing, and by means of which he ascends to fuller knowledge of God. Between certain of them we shall find three deflections from the pathway into which the divine will would have led him; deflections which delayed the purposes of God in his life, and which brought to him deep sorrow and burning shame.

Before we enter upon the examination of these manifestations, let me remind you that the God of Abraham is our God and Father in Christ; that His ways with Abraham are illustrations of His ways with us; and that the measure in which, like Abraham, we obey His commands, is precisely the measure in which He will manifest Himself to our hearts. "He that hath My commandments and keepeth them, he it is that loveth Me; and he that loveth Me shall be loved of My Father; and I will love him, and will manifest Myself to him" (John 14. 21. For a fuller explanation of the Saviour's meaning see verses 23 and 24).

First Manifestation: *"Get thee out"* (*Genesis* 12. 1)

"Now the Lord had said unto Abram, get thee out of thy country, and from thy kindred, and from thy father's house, unto a land that I will shew thee" (Genesis 12. 1).

A comparison of these words with Genesis 11. 31 and Acts 7. 2-4 explains a great deal and conveys a solemn lesson. Stephen declares that "the God of glory appeared unto Abraham when he was in Mesopotamia, before he dwelt in Haran" and said to him the words contained in

Genesis 12. 1. Moreover it was to Abram alone that the call was addressed (Isaiah 51. 2). But instead of going on to the land to which God had called him—which was quite evidently Canaan—he came to Haran, the most northerly town of the Chaldean empire, and dwelt there (Genesis 11. 31). And instead of taking with him only his wife, the one other person included in the call, he was accompanied by his father and his nephew Lot. It seems clear, therefore, that the ties of nature thus prevented Abram from rendering full obedience to the divine command; and Stephen goes on to say that it was only after these ties were severed that he did so. "Abram came to Haran; and from thence, when his father was dead, he removed him into this land wherein ye now dwell" (Acts 7. 4).

These facts explain the tense of the verb in Genesis 12. 1. "The Lord *had* said unto Abram get thee out . . . from . . . unto a land that I will shew thee"; for until Abram had rendered obedience to that command, until he acted up to the light which he had, God had nothing further to say to him.

A solemn principle finds illustration here. If there is anything in God's Word to which we are consciously disobedient, further communication from God is impossible so long as the disobedience continues. You may read your Bible, and give of your substance and your time; but these are no substitutes for obedience. "To obey is better than sacrifice, and to hearken than the fat of rams" (1 Samuel 15. 22).

In inimitable patience God waited for his chosen man; and in contrast to the first setting out from the Chaldean home, of which it is written that "they went forth from Ur of the Chaldees to go into the land of Canaan, and they came unto Haran and dwelt there," it is now stated that Abraham and his household "went forth to go into the land of Canaan and into the land of Cannan they came" (Genesis 12. 5). At last he is in the place to which he was originally called.

It should be noted that God's command was accompanied, not with reasons, but with promises. "To give His reason would be to propose discussion; but to give a promise is to show that the reason though undisclosed is all-sufficient; for in the case of the Allwise a promise is the harvest, of which a reason would be but the bare seed" (Matthew 19. 21; Mark 10. 29-30; Acts 16. 31; 2 Corinthians 6. 17-18). In reality we have nothing to do with the reasons upon which God's commands are founded. We are to walk by faith, not by sight. To have faith in God is to comprehend all reasons in one act. The command to Abram was: "get thee out from thy country, and from thy kindred, and from thy father's house"; and the promise was: (1) that God would make of him a great nation to compensate him for the one which he had relinquished; (2) that Heaven's blessing would rest on him personally to compensate him for the loss of kindred; and (3) that for the loss of his father's house, God would recompense him by making him the founder of a new house—the house of Israel (Acts 2. 36). Beyond these personal and material blessings there were the spiritual ones: "Thou shalt be a blessing . . . and in thee shall all families of the earth be blessed."

Second Manifestation: "I will give" (Genesis 12. 7)

Having now come to the land to which he had been called, Abram's faith is honoured and his obedience rewarded by a second manifestation of Jehovah. "The Lord appeared unto him and said: unto thy seed will I give this land" (Genesis 12. 7). At the first manifestation he was merely assured that he would be shown the land (chapter 12. 1); now Jehovah said: "unto thy seed I will give this land." Abraham's response was threefold: (1) he builded an altar (verse 7) thereby testifying to the Canaanite that he was a worshipper of the true God; (2) he pitched his tent (verse 8) thereby declaring that he recognised that here he had no continuing city (Hebrews

11. 13-14); and (3) he called upon the name of the Lord (verse 8) thereby evidencing his reliance upon the divine protection from the enemies by whom he was surrounded.

These three things—worship, pilgrimage, prayer—are the distinctive marks of all who, like Abram, look for a city which hath foundations, whose builder and maker is God. The altar signifies that their worship is based upon sacrifice; the tent, that this is not their final home; and prayer, that the name of the Lord is a strong tower, into which the righteous may run and be safe (Proverbs 18. 10).

It should be noted that he builded his altar, but merely pitched his tent. His house was a slender bit of fluttering canvas; the place where he met and worshipped God was built with care.

First Deflection: Down to Egypt (Genesis 12. 10-20)

We saw that the ties of nature hindered Abram from coming into the land; we are now to see that the pangs of hunger drove him out of it. "There was a famine in the land; and Abram went down into Egypt to sojourn there" (verse 10).

Chaldea, the great world power in the north, out of which Abram was called, was the land in which they worshipped false gods (Joshua 24. 2-15); Egypt, the great world power in the south, into which he descended, was the land in which they were independent of God. The inhabitants of Egypt, instead of looking up for their supplies, looked down the valley of the Nile for them. Of this mighty stream—upon whose annual overflow their very existence depended—they boastingly said: "My river is my own; I have made it for myself" (Ezekiel 29. 3; compare Deuteronomy 11. 11). This first mention of Egypt, therefore, stamps it with the character which it ever afterwards assumes: it is a picture of the world which depends on its own resources, and in which men live as if God did not exist. The people of God are sternly forbidden to go down to Egypt; for the descent is usually not merely a geographical one, it is also a spiritual one (Isaiah 31. 1).

Now although Abram could trust God absolutely with his whole destiny, his faith failed in a particular circumstance of the process by which it was being wrought out; just as we, who trust God for the things of eternity, so frequently doubt Him for the things of time. During his stay in Egypt he ceased to be a worshipper of God—he had no altar; he lost his pilgrim character—he had no tent; and he called upon the king of Egypt for his needs instead of upon the name of the Lord. His faith failed (verse 10); his courage failed (verses 11-12); and in utter selfishness he sought his own safety, at the expense and danger of the one whom he loved best of all (verse 13). "How small great people can be; how weak strong men can be; how bad good people can be." By bitter experience he learned that a crust in Canaan with God is better than a feast in Egypt without Him.

Sarah, however, was an ancestress of Christ, and He saw that no evil befell her. He providentially intervened (verse 17) and she was released from the king's harem into which she had been taken (verses 14-20). In delivering her to her husband again, the heathen king practically said to Abraham: "There is the door; you may go" (verses 19-20). How inexpressibly sad!

The Return (Genesis 13. 1-4)

The atmosphere of Egypt had stifled faith; and glad indeed must Abram have been on the day in which he turned his back upon it. "Abram went up out of Egypt . . . and he went on his journeys . . . unto the place where his tent had been *at the beginning* . . . unto the place of the altar which he had made there at the first, and there Abram called on the name of the Lord (verses 1-4). He is back once more to the old conditions of fellowship with God—worship, pilgrimage, prayer. From the story of this declension two great and solemn principles emerge: (1) that all time spent out of fellowship with God is lost time; and (2) that a backslider gets right exactly at the place where he went wrong.

Chapter Sixteen

ABRAHAM (3)

Third Manifestation: *"Lift thine eyes"*
(*Genesis* 13. 14)

WHILE they were in Egypt, both Abraham and Lot acquired great wealth (chapter 13. 2, 5); and on their return to Canaan it was found that the land was unable to sustain their flocks that they might dwell together—a fact which led to quarrelling among the servants (verse 7). The story which follows is in five sections.

1. The Dangers of Riches (Verses 5-7)

It is a striking fact that money was the first cause of trouble after the Israelites entered Canaan (Joshua 7. 21) and after the commencement of the Christian church (Acts 5). Since the love of it increases with the increase of the money itself, the only way to escape from the snares which it brings is to regard it as a sacred trust from God of which an account will one day have to be rendered to Him.

2. The Generosity of Abraham (Verses 8, 9)

Seeing that separation was inevitable, but wishing to avoid strife in the presence of the heathen, Abram with princely magnanimity allowed Lot to have his choice of the whole land—an action in which God's chosen man reveals the graces of humility, peaceableness, unselfishness, and open-handed generosity. The man of faith is ever the man of the large heart. The language of Abram's soul was: "God will choose my inheritance for me" (Psalm 47. 4).

3. The Selfishness of Lot (Verses 10-13)

Swayed entirely by considerations of personal advantage, Lot lifted up his eyes and chose what in his judgment was the most highly favoured portion of the land. In his choice of the plain of Jordan he was also guided by the fact that it resembled the land of Egypt—the land in which he had so rapidly accumulated his wealth. It was the first step on to a path that led to irretrievable disaster.

4. The Message from Heaven (Verses 14-17)

At last Abram has fulfilled to the letter the original command to get out from his country, his kindred, and his father's house; and after Lot's departure we read immediately of the third manifestation of Jehovah to Abram. "The Lord said unto Abram, after that Lot was separated from him: Lift up now thine eyes, and look from the place where thou art northward, and southward, and eastward, and westward; for all the land which thou seest, to thee will I give it, and to thy seed forever" (verse 14); and then follow the promises of all the land (verse 15) and of an innumerable seed (verse 16). How true it is that

> "He gives the very best to those
> Who leave the choice with Him."

It should be noted that on every occasion on which God makes promise to Abram, He adds to what He promised before. Thus in chapter 12. 1-2, He says: "I will shew you the land"; in chapter 12. 7, "unto thy seed will I give this land"; and in chapter 13. 15, that He gives the land to Abram in its entirety and forever.

Observe the order of these verses: vision (verse 14); promise (verses 15-16); exhortation (verse 17).

5. The Blessedness of Fellowship (Verse 18)

Then Abram — separated from all earthly ties —

"removed his tent, and came and dwelt in the plain of Mamre, which is in Hebron, and built there an altar unto the Lord." Names in Scripture are full of significance. Hebron means fellowship; Mamre means fruitfulness; Judah—among whose mountains Hebron lay (Joshua 20. 7)—means praise. The order is true to Christian experience—separation, fellowship, fruitfulness, praise.

Fourth Manifestation: "Fear thou not"
(Genesis 14 and 15)

In the 14th chapter of Genesis we have the first recorded war in history; and it is an interesting fact that there are in the British Museum to-day, bricks that prove the existence of the kings here mentioned at the time to which this chapter refers. Our interest in the matter is spiritual rather than historical; for there are circumstances connected with the campaign which illustrate principles of abiding value for every Christian heart.

Lot, who, when he separated from Abram merely pitched his tent toward Sodom (chapter 13. 12), eventually took up his abode within its polluted walls (chapter 14. 12); and when it was attacked and overthrown by Chedorlaomer, the greatest conqueror of his age, Lot was among the prisoners of war.

Abraham, who had been enjoying halcyon days of fellowship with God among the mountains of Judah, was informed of his relative's distress; and, leaving his happy retreat in Hebron, proved himself a man of action as well as a worshipper of God; a soldier as well as a pilgrim. He, who was a lamb where his own interests were concerned, became a lion when acting on behalf of others. By a skilfully arranged and brilliantly executed night attack he threw the invading force into utter confusion, and we behold him returning from the conflict crowned with success and laden with spoil (verses 1 to 16).

On his way back to Hebron—the place of fellowship where he dwelt—he was met by two kings: Melchizedek king of Salem, and Bera king of Sodom. The remainder of the chapter—verse 17 to verse 24—describes his interviews with these two men.

Melchizedek (verses 18-20)

This mysterious personage is mentioned three times in Scripture: in Genesis 14, historically, in Psalm 110, prophetically; and in Hebrews 5 to 7, doctrinally. The writer to the Hebrews bids us consider how great this man was (Hebrews 7. 1-4), for he united the dignity of kingship with the sanctity of priesthood. He brought to Abram bread to sustain and wine to refresh (verse 18); and Abram bows before him as in the presence of a superior and received his blessing (verse 19-20).

The king of Sodom (verses 21-24)

Turning from Melchizedek—type of the Son of God Who shall one day be a priest upon His throne (Hebrews 7. 4; Zechariah 6. 13)—Abram now faces Bera king of Sodom; and at once his manner changes. He is conscious that he is no longer in the presence of a superior, but in that of a wicked man; and with courteous dignity he refuses to receive even a thread from Sodom's unrighteous king (verses 21-24). This leads directly to the fourth manifestation of Jehovah.

"After these things"—the things recorded in chapter 14—"the word of the Lord came to Abram in a vision saying: Fear not Abram: I am thy shield and thy exceeding great reward" (Genesis 15. 1). The exhortation, "Fear not, Abram, I am thy shield," was God's gracious way of hushing any fears of reprisal which might arise in His servant's heart; the assurance, "I am thy exceeding great reward," was heaven's infinite compensation to him for his refusal to be enriched at the hands of ungodly men. There was to be no fear, no danger, no loss.

To gather up some of the lessons of the chapter:

1. There is a fight of faith as well as a rest of faith.

2. The secret place of fellowship with God is the starting point for victory.

3. Only those who habitually dwell there can be of service in any emergency.

4. Faith makes us independent of man, but not indifferent to his needs and sorrows.

5. Faith makes us chivalrous (verse 14), disinterested (verse 22), and unworldly (verse 23).

6. The way of earthly renunciation is the way of heavenly gain.

7. God is our refuge, our resource, and our reward (Genesis 15. 1).

Genesis 15. 2-21

The fourth manifestation of Jehovah to Abram, and the assurances of protection and reward which accompanied it, lifted him to a new level. His knowledge of God is now so great that he can speak freely to Him of the fear that ever lurked in his heart. Ten years had passed since he entered into Canaan and still he has no son to inherit his name and destiny (verses 2-3). He has God's word that he will inherit the land of Canaan; but now he asks for a sign whereby he may know that he shall inherit it (verse 8).

In response to these questionings God reaffirms that he shall have a son and heir (verse 4); enters into covenant with His friend (verses 9-12); and, after outlining the the history of Abram's descendants for 400 years (verses 13-16), gives two symbols which describe their chequered career (verse 17). Finally, He defines the limits of the land which would eventually be theirs (verses 18-21).

Note 1. The great words of Genesis 15. 6 are quoted three times in the New Testament: in Romans 4. 3 where the emphasis is on the word "counted"; in Galatians 3. 6

where the emphasis is on the word "believed"; and in James 2. 23 where the emphasis is on the word "righteousness."

Note 2. Verse 13 speaks of exile, bondage, and affliction; verse 14, of deliverance; and verse 16 of possession. These five words exactly describe Israel's history as set forth in detail in the Scripture—Genesis 46. to Joshua 4.

Second Deflection: The Egyptian maid (Genesis 16)

The epistle to the Hebrews declares that it is through faith and patience that we inherit the promises (chapter 6. 12); but in the story before us we learn that while Abram possessed faith (chapter 15) he lacked patience (chapter 16). He believed in God, but could not wait for God. That impatience led to a disaster, the effects of which abide to this day. The episode is in three sections:

(1) THE IMPATIENCE OF ABRAM (VERSES 1-6)

This consisted in his acquiescence in a fleshly expedient to realise the promise, and hasten the purposes of God.

While the suggestion of Sarah on this occasion (verse 2) seems to us strange and unnatural, archaeological discoveries show that she was acting on what was a common custom at the time. For the code of Hammurabi—the mighty king who reigned over Babylon in the days of Abraham—distinctly allows a married woman to do what Sarah here did, (Law no. 144). Not only so; the same Code—Law no. 146—allows the mistress to reduce the maid so given, to the position of a slave again; and while it seems to us that Abraham acted unfairly to Hagar (verse 6), he was in fact only conceding to Sarah what was her absolute right by Babylonian law.

On the other hand, whatever Babylonian law may have allowed, the purpose of God in marriage was monogamy (Genesis 2); and this departure from the divine ideal involved all three of them in sorrow. Insolence in Hagar (verse 4) produced jealousy in Sarah (verse 5); and jealousy proved itself as cruel as the grave (verse 6; Song of Solomon 8. 6). The home of the friend of God—once the abode of peace—became one of bitter and unending strife; and Hagar, unable to endure the hatred of her angry mistress, anticipated the wise man's advice and fled to the wilderness (Proverbs 21. 19).

Three lessons emerge:

(1) There is such a thing as the discipline of delay.

(2) Right ends do not justify wrong means.

(3) Human expedients can never further the purposes of God.

(2) THE TENDERNESS OF GOD (VERSES 7-14)

If man had treated this proud-spirited girl with harshness, the angel of the Lord showed her the most exquisite kindness. He counsels the wanderer to return and submit (verse 9), cheering her with a wonderful promise (verse 10).

She responds to the kindness of God with words that have been sadly misunderstood (verse 13). "Thou God seest me" are words which you will sometimes find on the walls of Sunday schools with a fiery glaring eye underneath them, giving the impression that God is a great detective. They were originally used by a lonely, friendless girl who, in her distress, was found by One Who treated her with the utmost tenderness. They form the basis of a living creed (2 Chronicles 16. 9), and are at once the surest and most effective restraint from vice, the safest and most powerful incentive to virtue.

(3) THE FAR-REACHING CONSEQUENCES OF SIN (VERSES 15-16)

Hagar was an Egyptian maid. She doubtless had joined Abram's household when he had deflected from the path of the divine will, and she accompanied him on his return to Canaan. Behold the far-reaching effects of that one false step of this man of God. Ishmael, the son of Hagar by Abram, was the progenitor of the Arabians. Had Abram never departed from God he would never have entered Egypt; had he never entered Egypt he would never have met Hagar; had he never met Hagar there would have been no Moslem question—the blight and curse of Islam.

> "O mortal man of one false step beware,
> For one false step may bring an age of care."

CHAPTER SEVENTEEN

ABRAHAM (4)

Fifth Manifestation: *"Walk before Me"* (*Genesis* 17)
(1) RESTORATION (VERSES 1-3)

BY ignoring the chapter divisions and reading 16. 16 and 17. 1 together we learn a solemn lesson. "Abram was fourscore and six years old, when Hagar bare Ishmael to Abram. And when Abram was ninety years old and nine, the Lord appeared to Abram." That is to say, that for at least thirteen slow moving years there had been absolute silence between God and Abram—silence which must have been more terrible to God's servant than the most solemn rebuke. His unbelief and impatience in the matter of Hagar had shut God out from his vision; for God will not reveal Himself where He is not trusted.

As always, however, it was God Who broke the silence. "The Lord appeared unto Abram and said unto him: I am the Almighty God; walk before Me and be thou perfect." It is a practical illustration of Psalm 23. 3: "He restoreth my soul; He leadeth me in the paths of righteousness for His name's sake."

In Genesis 17. 1 we have a revelation and a command. The revelation is: "I am the Almighty God"—a name which speaks of One Who has limitless power and is infinite in resource. With much tenderness God thus lays His finger on that which occasioned the long silence between Him and His friend, and clearly indicates that behind every promise which He had made, lay Omnipotence to guarantee its fulfilment.

It should be carefully noted that this title of God reappears in one of Paul's epistles, and that there a relationship is linked with it such as Abram never knew.

"I will receive you and will be a Father unto you, and ye shall be My sons and daughters saith the Lord Almighty" (2 Corinthians 6. 17-18). It is the union of Fatherhood and Omnipotence.

The inevitable happened: "Abram fell on his face" (verse 3). The goodness of God humbled him to the dust and led him to repentance.

In the light of the revelation, the command becomes gloriously possible: "Walk before Me and be thou perfect" —upright, sincere, true. This does not mean what is known as sinless perfection—a doctrine which would necessitate perfect knowledge and moral completeness, neither of which we shall possess in this world. The doctrine which I have named is orthodoxy in a hurry; for one of the holiest men that ever lived had to say at the end of his career: "Not as though I had already attained, either were already perfect; but I follow after, if that I may apprehend that for which also I am apprehended of Christ Jesus" (Philippians 3.12).

(2) COVENANT (VERSES 4-8)

The original promise is again expanded (verse 6); and the name of God's servant is changed from Abram, which means "exalted father", to Abraham, which means "father of a multitude" in order to correspond with the expansion (verse 5). Study the "I will's" of verses 6, 7 and 8.

(3) CIRCUMCISION (VERSES 9-14)

This rite was the token of the covenant which God made with Abraham (verse 10). Later on it became a synonym for the Israelites in contrast to the nations among whom they dwelt (Judges 14. 3; Acts 11. 2-3). Spiritually it signifies the putting off the body of the flesh by all who have died and are risen with Christ (Colossians 2. 11-12).

Sarah (verses 15-22)

Sarah is now for the first time specifically mentioned as the mother of the promised heir (verses 15, 16), although had Abraham not been confused by Babylonian laws he would have known this all along. The divine ideal of one man, and one woman, and absolute loyalty to each other while life shall last, would have ruled out of court the Hagar expedient. Verses 17-18 indicate that Abraham laughed incredulously at the promise of God; and it is noticeable that God did not discuss the matter with him but merely reiterated His promise (verse 19). The affections of the old man had entwined themselves around Ishmael; and God goes on to show that although Ishmael was not the heir, he too would be richly blessed (verses 20-21).

Obedience (verses 23-27)

The fifth communication from Heaven is now ended (verse 22); and Abraham hastens to render obedience to God's command to circumcise. That obedience was characterised by two things: promptitude—"the self-same day" (verse 26); and completeness—all the men of his house were circumcised with him (verse 27).

Sixth Manifestation: "Strong in faith" (Genesis 18)

Ignoring again the chapter divisions we find that obedience to the divine command brought Abraham another manifestation of Jehovah. "In the self-same day . . . Abraham and Ishmael and all the men of his house were circumcised. And the Lord appeared unto Abraham in the plains of Mamre" (Genesis 17. 26 to 18. 1).

Before we examine the details of this sixth communication from Heaven, it may be of interest to say a few words regarding the Person Who in this chapter is nine times called "the Lord". He received the worship of Abraham (verse 2); He promised to do that which God alone can do—bring life out of death (verses 10-11); He exercised divine prerogatives (verse 21); and is addressed as "the Judge of all the earth" (verse 25). While the New Testament distinctly affirms that God in His essential Being has never been seen (John 1. 18; 1 Timothy 1. 17), Genesis 18 is equally explicit that there was on that occasion a pre-incarnate unveiling of Jehovah Who is the second Person of the Trinity and Who ultimately became God manifest in the flesh (1 Timothy 3. 16).

Abraham is still on the heights of Mamre, and just as in chapter 14 we saw him leaving his retreat to act on behalf of the inhabitants of the doomed cities, so here we find him doing so to intercede for them. The chapter is in three sections.

(1) HOSPITALITY (VERSES 1-8)

The picture drawn in these verses is a beautiful one. Abraham is shown to be courteous (verses 2-3), practical (verses 4-5), hospitable (verses 6-7), respectful (verse 8).

(2) FELLOWSHIP (VERSES 9-22)

The tenth verse is an unveiling of Omnipotence. The incredulity of Sarah (verses 11-13) elicited one of those statements which are repeated in various ways in the book of God—statements which enable the believer to laugh at impossibilities and to affirm that they shall be done (Genesis 18. 14; Job 42. 2; Jeremiah 32. 17-27; Luke 1. 37; Ephesians 3. 20-21).

And now we come to an incident in which Abraham stands revealed as the friend of God. One of the special privileges of friendship is the communication of secrets; and Abraham is here granted that special privilege (verses 16 to 21; Psalm 25. 14; Amos 3. 7; John 15. 15).

(3) INTERCESSION (VERSES 22-23)

It would seem that at this point the two angels moved away, and very shortly afterwards entered Sodom (chapter 19. 1). "The men turned their faces towards Sodom; but Abraham stood yet before the Lord." And then follows the record of the first great intercessory prayer of the Bible in which are brought before us some of the things which will characterise all true intercession. They are at least seven in number; communion (verse 33); faith (verse 25); humility (verse 27); unselfishness (verse 23); earnestness (verse 30); perseverance (verse 32); compassion (verse 24).

Lot (Genesis 19)

In this chapter we behold the deepest depths of human iniquity and depravity; and in Ezekiel 16. 49 we find the main features of the path by which these depths were reached—"fulness of bread and abundance of idleness." In the presence of the appalling wickedness which the messengers of God found there, we feel instinctively that, in overwhelming the guilty city with swift and irretrievable disaster, God did that which was right (chapter 18. 25). While it is true that to-day "the wrath of God is revealed against *all* ungodliness and unrighteousness of men" (Romans 1. 18), history makes it clear that in the course of the centuries God has made examples of certain lands and cities, just as He did of the cities of the plain (Jude 7); and that in so doing He was merely acting on the principle of the landlord who "ejects bad tenants". Our interest in the story is confined to Lot, the central figure in it.

(1) There are certain facts about this man which give us the key to his character. (a) Three times it is said that he went with Abraham (Genesis 12. 4; 13. 1; 13. 5). That is to say, he went with the man who went with God. His faith was, therefore, a kind of second hand faith. (b)

Nevertheless that faith was genuine for he is called "just Lot—that righteous man" (2 Peter 2. 7-8). (c) But although, like Abraham, he believed in the Lord and it was counted unto him for righteousness, there is not a single deed of faith to his credit: his name does not appear in Hebrews 11—the Westminster Abbey of the Bible.

(2) The stages by which he reached the position in which the angels found him are clearly marked. (a) He pitched his tent towards Sodom (chapter 13. 12); (b) he dwelt in Sodom (chapter 14. 12); (c) he became chief citizen of Sodom (chapter 19. 1). These stages illustrate the saying that as a rule men do not plunge into iniquity; they glide into it. They are "like the swimmer who ventures into the outmost circles of the whirlpool and who ends at last in its vortex."

(3) From the day on which he entered Sodom he never enjoyed a happy hour. Peter tells us (2 Peter 2. 7) that that righteous man dwelling among them . . . "vexed his righteous soul from day to day with their unlawful deeds"; and it is an appalling fact that the word there translated "vexed" is the same word as in Revelation 20. 10, is translated "tormented". "The devil . . . shall be tormented day and night for ever." Lot's life in Sodom was literally hell upon earth.

(4) Not only did he lose his joy, he lost his testimony. When judgment was announced and he sought to warn his relatives of the impending doom, "he seemed as one that mocked unto his sons in law" (verse 14). What he gained in worldly influence he lost in spiritual power.

(5) He was burned out of Sodom (verses 15 to 20). Probably the Bible contains no more concrete example, worked out into its minutest detail, of the great New Testament truth: "If any man's (disciple's) work shall be burned, he shall suffer loss; but himself shall be saved; yet so as through fire" (1 Corinthians 3. 15)—"escaping from a burning ruin down a corridor of flame. Lot entered

Sodom a man of substance, he leaves it a pauper; he entered it a prince, he leaves it a fugitive; he flees from falling lightnings which consume the architecture of a lifetime."

(6) The final act in the drama sets down in letters of living flame that the evil that men do, lives after them. For under the influence of wine he dishonours his own daughters, and becomes by means of them, the progenitor of the Moabites and the Ammonites, who proved to be the most relentless enemies of the people of God (verses 30-38).

(7) The believer has three great enemies: the world, the flesh, and the devil; and Scripture has an outstanding example of failure before each of them. David fell before the flesh (2 Samuel 11); Peter, before the devil (Matthew 26); and Lot—whose New Testament counterpart is Demas—before the world (Genesis 19; 2 Timothy 4. 10). David was restored; Peter was restored; neither Lot nor Demas was restored; they passed into eternity under a cloud. The very enormity of their sins brought David and Peter to the feet of their God in humble penitence. But the descent to worldliness is like the freezing of ice on a pond—an almost unperceived process; it resembles those habits, sometimes acquired, which are too insignificant to be noticed until they become too strong to be broken.

Chapter Eighteen

ABRAHAM (5)

Third Deflection of Abraham: In Abimelech's Land
(Genesis 20)

THE outstanding lesson which we learn from this third
deflection of Abraham may be set forth in a couplet
from George Herbert:

"Dare to be true, nothing can need a lie;
The fault which needs it most, grows two thereby."

It appears from the narrative that, between Abraham
and Sarah, whose beauty fascinated kings, an arrangement
had been made before they left Mesopotamia whereby
she was, in the presence of strangers, to pose as his sister
instead of as his wife (verse 13); and although they had
had one solemn warning of the danger of such an expedient
(chapter 12) we find them here again acting upon it. We
learn the sad fact that a believer who, when walking with
God, can rise to rare heights of dignity and nobleness can,
if he forsakes that path, descend to depths lower than do
worldly men. "Abraham's fall on this occasion was deeper
than on the previous one; for he now had the divine
promise that within that very year Sarah would become
the mother of a miraculous child."

From another point of view the incident was clearly a
fresh attempt on the part of Satan to render invalid the
promise with regard to the coming Messianic seed (see
Genesis 3. 15; Exodus 1. 16-22; 2 Chronicles 22. 10-11;
Matthew 2. 16-18). So unreliable are even the best of
men, and so bitter Satan's hatred of Christ, that if God
had not intervened again and again that promise would
never have been fulfilled (Psalm 105. 13-15).

The man who so powerfully interceded for Sodom here
leaves the place of fellowship; and that sacred ministry

temporarily ceases. It is clear that the exercise of soul through which God caused Abraham to pass because of his deviation from the path of rectitude, not only effected his complete restoration, but also led him out once more in intercession on behalf of the man whom he had wronged (chapter 20. 7 and 17). Abraham's three deflections therefore "represent the vulnerable points in the life of faith. The first blow is directed against a separated walk, the second against trust in the Word; the third against prayer. The devil always concentrates his assaults on these three citadels of sainthood."

Seventh Manifestation: Cast him out (Genesis 21)

This chapter is in four sections:

1. The birth of Isaac (verses 1 to 8).
2. The departure of Ishmael (verses 9 to 14).
3. The kindness of God (verses 14 to 21).
4. Abraham and Abimelech (verses 22 to 34).

In due course the promise of God was fulfilled; and the opening verses of Genesis 21 tell of the supreme gladness with which Isaac was welcomed by Sarah and Abraham. Formerly, when the promise was made that she should have a son, Sarah had laughed incredulously (chapter 18. 10-12); now she laughs for sheer joy because the promise has been translated into fact (chapter 21. 6).

In the midst of their joy, however, Ishmael was found mocking or persecuting Isaac (verse 9; Galatians 4. 29); and Sarah peremptorily demanded that Hagar and her son be expelled from the home. "Wherefore she said unto Abraham: cast out this bondwoman and her son: for the son of this bondwoman shall not be heir with my son, even with Isaac. And the thing was very grievous in Abraham's sight because of his son" (verses 9-11).

But when Abraham was thus brought very low God appeared unto him; and on this, the seventh manifestation of Himself to His servant, brought him counsel in his perplexity, and comfort to sustain him in his sorrow. He was not to grieve unnecessarily over Hagar and Ishmael (verse 12); he was to accede to Sarah's request, for it was in Isaac that the Messianic line ran (verse 12); and he was assured that Ishmael, too, would become a mighty man "because he was Abraham's seed" (verse 13).

Genesis 21 should be carefully compared with Galatians 4. The historical facts recorded in the former are said in the latter to be full of spiritual significance. Sarah and Hagar—the two mothers—represent grace and law respectively. Isaac and Ishmael—the two sons—represent the two natures in the child of God (Galatians 4. 29). "He that was born after the flesh" typifies the old man which we are to put off (Ephesians 4. 22); "he that was born after the spirit" represents the new man which we are to put on (Ephesians 4. 24; see also Galatians 5. 16-18).

Eighth Manifestation: *Take thy son* (*Genesis* 22)

We have seen that the two great controlling principles in Abraham's life were faith and obedience; and in the chapter before us now we have the supreme illustration of the effects on the earthly side of these two principles, namely, surrender. In chapter 12 Abraham abandoned home and country; in chapter 13 he relinquished, in favour of Lot, his right to the first claim of the land; in chapter 14 he renounced the offer of the king of Sodom; in chapter 21 he gave up Ishmael; in chapter 22 he surrendered Isaac. There are four things in the last-named chapter which we are to note.

(1) HEAVY TRIAL (VERSES 1-2)

"And it came to pass . . . that God did tempt Abraham." The word translated "tempt" means "to prove," and is so translated in the R.V. (see also I Kings 10. 1; 1 Samuel 17.39). "Satan tempts us that he may bring out the evil that is in our hearts; God tries or tests us that He may bring out all the good."

"God did prove Abraham and said unto him: Abraham; and he said: Behold, here am I. And He said: Take now thy son, thine only son Isaac whom thou lovest, and get thee into the land of Moriah; and offer him there for a burnt offering upon one of the mountains which I will tell thee of" (verses 1-2).

It may be well at the outset to answer a difficulty which distresses some tender hearts. "God seems to have required of Abraham what was wrong: He seems to sanction human sacrifice. My reply is: God did not sanction it. You must take the story as a whole—the conclusion as well as the commencement. The sacrifice of Isaac was commanded at first, and forbidden at the end. Had it ended in Abraham's accomplishing the sacrifice, I know not what could have been said; it would have left on the page of Scripture a dark and painful blot." But He Who said: Take thy son and offer him (verse 2) said also: Lay not thine hand upon the lad (verse 12). It was Abraham's heart, not Isaac's life, that God wanted, and He got it. Let me illustrate.

It is said that during the Napoleonic wars the Emperors of Prussia, Austria, and Russia, were discussing the relative absolute unquestioning obedience of their soldiers —each claiming in this regard the pre-eminence for his own soldiers. They were sitting in a room in the second storey. To test the matter they agreed that each would call in turn the sentinel at the door and command him to leap out at the window.

First the Prussian monarch called his man: "Leap out of the window" was the order. "Your Majesty," said the soldier, "it would kill me." He was then dismissed, and the Austrian soldier was called. "Leap out of the window," commanded the Emperor. "I will," said the man, "if you really mean what you say." He was dismissed, and the Czar called his man. "Leap out of that window," said the Czar. Without a word in reply the man crossed himself and started to obey; but, of course, was stopped before he reached the window. Were these Emperors guilty of murder? asks the narrator of the story. Surely not; because their purpose was not to sacrifice the soldiers but only to test their obedience. God's purpose likewise must be judged not by His command alone but by the story of Genesis 22 in its completeness.

The words of verse 2 have been compared to a case of knives lacerating Abraham's heart. They contain a command, obedience to which would to all appearance have rendered invalid the promise of God; for it was in Isaac that the seed was to be called. Here then we have the greatest of the men of faith subjected to the heaviest of all forms of trial.

(2) Swift Obedience (Verses 3-10)

Abraham's response to the command was (a) Swift. "Abraham rose up early in the morning"; he made haste and delayed not to keep God's commandment (Psalm 119. 60). (b) Unquestioning. He had already obeyed when he knew not where; he now obeys when he knew not why. (c) Deliberate. No sudden flicker of enthusiasm was this, but patient, persevering, unwavering obedience through the slow-moving hours of three leaden-footed days. (d) Complete. "Abraham stretched forth his hand and took the knife to slay his son" (verse 10).

His abandonment to the will of God has now been proved genuine and unreserved; and in verses 16-18 God speaks of him as having actually done that which he was commanded to do. "By Myself have I sworn, saith the Lord; for because thou hast done this thing and hast not withheld thy son, thine only son, that in blessing I will bless thee . . . and in thy seed shall all the nations of the earth be blessed; because thou hast obeyed My voice." "By faith Abraham when he was tried offered up Isaac" (Hebrews 11. 17).

It is noticeable that there is not a word said about Abraham's feelings during this terrible ordeal. The innocent question of Isaac (verse 7) must have been to his father as a furnace heated seven times. "He looks on his child and there is agony. He looks up to his God, and the agony melts into the calm of unruffled peace." It is clear both from Genesis 22 and Hebrews 11 that he was quite convinced that if Isaac were offered in obedience to divine command, God would have raised him again from the dead. Before parting from the servants at the foot of Moriah he said to them: "I and the lad will go yonder and worship and come again to you" (verse 5); and commenting on the story Hebrews 11. 19 definitely states that he accounted "that God was able to raise him up even from the dead, from whence also he received him in a figure."

(3) DIVINE MANIFESTATION (VERSES 11-14)

The eighth manifestation of Jehovah to Abraham is of a threefold character. In the first portion of it He proves Abraham (verses 1-2); in the second, He restrains him (verses 11-14); and in the third, He rewards him (verses 15-18).

The contents of this precious portion—the typical significance of which we shall examine later—may be set forth in the words of the poet:

"Say not, dear soul, from whence can God relieve thy care?
Remember that Omnipotence hath servants everywhere.
His methods are sublime, His ways supremely kind,
God never is before His time and never is behind."

His intervention on behalf of His sorely-tried friend was absolutely in the nick of time (verses 11-12); and the thorn-crowned ram became the servant of Omnipotence, which Abraham took and offered for a burnt-offering in the stead of his son (verse 13). God had indeed for Abraham made a way of escape (1 Corinthians 10. 13).

"And Abraham called the name of that place Jehovah-jireh," that is: "The Lord will see, or, the Lord will provide" (Genesis 22. 14 margin). "By combining the thoughts suggested by the two readings we grasp the tremendous truth that the God of vision is the God of provision. The foresight and omnipotence of God are two wings of an eagle that soars into the empyrean bearing Abraham upon its pinions."

(4) MEASURELESS REWARD (VERSES 15-19)

Abraham's perfect obedience brings heaven's measureless reward. "Supreme sacrifice is crowned with rapturous blessing. God has purposes so gracious and promises so generous that the grandest similes are required to express them. The form as well as the contents of the promise is exuberant. Elect to unexampled suffering, Abraham was also elect to unexampled blessing."

To Abraham personally the blessing was one which resulted in deepened and matured knowledge of God, and of the heart-rest which that brings. "I find," says Tholuck, "in all Christians who have passed through much tribulation, a certain quality of ripeness which I am of the opinion can be found in no other school. Just as a certain degree of solar heat is necessary to bring the finest fruits to perfection, so is fiery trial indispensable for ripening the inner man."

The death of Sarah (Genesis 23)

This chapter brings before us Abraham's supreme sorrow—the death of his beautiful wife. "Sarah died in Kirjath-arba . . . and Abraham came to mourn for Sarah and to weep for her" (verse 2). "The unspoken memories of a lifetime were in those tears." Faith in God does not lead to stoical indifference in the presence of sorrow, although it restrains us from sorrowing as others who have no hope. It "neither eradicates nor reproves sorrow, but tempers and hallows it and binds up the broken heart."

The loneliness which characterised his life after Sarah's death deepened in his heart the consciousness of the fact that he was a stranger and sojourner on the earth (verse 4). That consciousness re-appears in his descendants again and again (Genesis 47. 9; Exodus 6. 4; 1 Chronicles 29. 15; Psalm 39. 12; Hebrews 11. 13).

The Call of Rebekah (Genesis 24)

This is one of the most charming love stories in the Bible. It records how, at the command of his master, the unnamed servant went forth to seek a bride for his master's son who had figuratively died and risen again. It describes how he came in touch with the woman who was divinely chosen for the well-beloved son; and how, with tales of Isaac's wealth and glory, he sought to detach her heart from the scene in which he found her. It tells of how the chosen bride was willing to leave all and to go to a land and a person that were known to her only by report, and of how that person came part of the way to meet her. It narrates, finally, how that one received her unto himself in order that she might share his home and destiny.

These historical facts teem with spiritual significance. For they illustrate in a very wonderful way the mission of the Holy Spirit Who has come to seek the church; and Who, by unfolding the personal and official glories of the risen Lord, detaches Christian hearts from the world and allures them on to One Whom having not seen they love.

Like Isaac, our Lord Jesus will come from His Father's house to meet us; like him, too, the Saviour will receive us unto Himself in order that we may share His royal home and glorious destiny for ever (1 Thessalonians 4; John 14; Colossians 3. 1; Revelation 22).

From another point of view the unnamed servant exemplifies in a sevenfold way what should characterise every true servant of God:

(1)   He did not run before he was sent; he was commissioned (verses 1-9).

(2)   He recognised his absolute dependence upon God: he was prayerful (verses 10-14).

(3)   He sought definite guidance and obtained it (verses 15-21).

(4)   His service was blended with worship (verses 22-28).

(5)   His master's interests were his one concern (verses 29-53).

(6)   His message was an urgent one and admitted of no delay (verses 54-60).

(7)   His task was not completed until he led to the son of his master the one whose heart he had won (verses 61-67).

From still another point of view—that of the soul-winner—the late William Thompson, the Scottish Evangelist, used the following beautiful outline:

1.   Sought prayerfully (verse 12).

2.   Captivated completely (verse 18).

3.   Enriched lavishly (verse 22).

4.   Brought jealously (verse 61).

5.   Delivered gladly (verse 66).

The Death of Abraham (Genesis 25)

"Abraham gave up the ghost . . . an old man and full of years; and was gathered to his people" (verse 8). That last phrase cannot mean that he was laid to rest with his people in Mesopotamia, for he was buried in the cave of Machpelah (verse 10). The gathering place was not in Chaldea but in the unseen world; and the phrase gives point to our Lord's word when He said that God is not the God of the dead but of the living (Matthew 22. 32).

"His sons Isaac and Ishmael buried him in the cave of

Machpelah" (verse 9). "Death brings estranged brothers together to drink the cup of a common sorrow; they look at each other with teardimmed eyes; they see, in the light of eternity, how paltry are all causes of earthly strife. When all other means of reconciliation fail, death makes friends and brethren kind."

As we think back through the chapters which describe the life of this great man of God we feel how true are Strachan's eloquent words: "Through God's loving kindness he had found good in everything. He was rich, and riches were not a curse to him; he suffered, and trial was a blessing to him; he sinned, and by God's wonderful grace, he got good out of evil."

Chapter Nineteen

ISAAC—SONSHIP

(1) Isaac Typically

WE pass now to Isaac who stands on the page of inspiration as the illustration of the truth of Sonship. Comparing what is said of him in Genesis 21 with what is said of him in Galatians 4, we learn that he is the type of those glad souls who, standing fast in the liberty wherewith Christ has set them free, are free indeed (Galatians 5. 1; John 8. 36). He is the son of the free-woman in contrast to Ishmael who was the son of the bondwoman (Galatians 4. 22); he was born after the spirit while the other was born after the flesh (Galatians 4. 29); and he was the true heir (Galatians 4. 30).

Three New Testament Scriptures sum up the spiritual teaching which underlies these historical facts, namely: John 1. 12; Galatians 4. 6; Hebrews 2. 10. The first of these tells us of the place of liberty into which we have been brought—that of sons; the second tells us of the power which enables us to live as sons—the Spirit of God; while the third unveils the prospect which lies ahead of us as sons—an inheritance of glory (see also 1 Peter 1. 3-5; Romans 8. 14-18).

(2) Isaac Personally

Personally, Isaac is the least interesting of the three patriarchs. Although he lived longer than Abraham or Jacob, much less space is devoted to him than to either of these. Apart from the story of his "obedience unto death" (Genesis 22), and the record of the birth and blessing of his two sons (Genesis 25 and 27), almost everything that is said of him is confined to one chapter—Genesis 26. He is there revealed to us as a man whose disposition was reflective rather than energetic; passive rather than active. "A lover of solitude he well knew the soothing influence of nature over vexed spirits. The moaning of the wind, the murmur of the fountain, the rustling of the grain possess to him inexpressible charm. A lover of quietude, he avoids din and conflict and devotes himself to peaceful pursuits—the sowing of the seed, the digging of wells."

In the last-named chapter we find two manifestations of Jehovah to him; the first being recorded in verses 2-5. Because of famine Isaac had evidently purposed to go down to Egypt—the granary of the ancient world; but on his way thither he was stopped at Gerar by Jehovah Who forbad his going to Egypt, and commanded him to stay where he was (verses 1-3). According to Genesis 10. 19 Gerar was on the borderland of Canaan, and was a kind of halfway house to Egypt. The descent (verses 1-6) was followed by deceit (verses 7-9)—Isaac doing in Gerar what his father did in Egypt. It was an act of cowardice and selfishness for which, but for the mercy of God, he would have had to pay dearly. Even as it was, his deceit was followed by disgrace (verses 10-11)—the conduct of the heathen king putting to shame the conduct of the believer.

Prosperity came to Isaac in Abimelech's land (verses 12-14) and this led to contention with Abimelech's men (verses 15-21). Only when "he removed from thence" did he find refreshment and rest (verse 22).

"And he went up from thence to Beersheba" (verse 23). He is now back to the land of God's appointment; and we read that the Lord appeared unto him the same night and, bidding him "Fear not," assured him of heavenly companionship, divine blessing, and abundant fruitfulness (verse 24).

In response to this second manifestation of Jehovah Isaac builded an altar there—worship; he called upon the name of the Lord—prayer; he pitched his tent there —pilgrimage; and there his servants digged a well—

refreshment (verse 25). "Here we have most blessed progress. The moment he took a step in the right direction, he went from strength to strength. He entered into the joy of God's presence, tasted the sweets of true worship, exhibited the character of a stranger and pilgrim, and found peaceful refreshment and an undisputed well, which the Philistines could not stop because they were not there."

The effect on others of his complete restoration to fellowship with his God is told in verses 26-33. Those who hitherto had striven with him now recognise that the Lord was manifestly with him (verses 27, 28); and, instead of seeking at every turn to antagonise him, earnestly desire his friendship (verse 29).

The Well: "We have found water" (Verse 32)

The Scriptures have much to say about wells and water. These two similes are employed to set forth:

(1) The emptiness of the ungodly life—2 Peter 2. 17: "Wells without water."

(2) The freshness of the Christian life—John 4. 14: "A well of living water."

(3) The cleansing effect of the Word—Ephesians 5. 26; Psalm 119. 9: "Cleanse and sanctify."

(4) The priceless privilege of prayer—Numbers 20. 8; Exodus 17. 6: "That rock was Christ" (1 Corinthians 10. 4). Smitten once; spoken to often.

(5) The fulness of the Spirit—Ephesians 5. 18; John 7. 37-39: Rivers of living water.

(6) The joy of the redeemed—Isaiah 12. 2-3: The wells of salvation.

(7) Complete and eternal satisfaction—Revelation 7. 13-17: "Fountains of living water."

Chapter Twenty

JACOB—DISCIPLINE

THE late Queen Victoria once visited a paper mill in the vicinity of Windsor Castle. The foreman showed the illustrious visitor over the works and pointed out the various stages through which the paper passed. Presently she was led into the rag-sorting shop where men were engaged in picking out rags from the refuse of the city. She enquired what was done with that dirty mess of rags and was told that, sorted out, it would make the finest white paper. Some little time afterwards Her Majesty received a packet of the most delicate white paper bearing her own image as a water-mark, and accompanying the gift was a letter explaining that the paper which she now saw before her was made from the rags which she had seen on the day of her visit.

This incident very aptly illustrates the transformation which took place in the life of Jacob whose story is now to engage our attention. When he first comes before us he is characterised by deceit, falsehood, cunning, and the most utter selfishness, and as we watch him in his dealings with his fellow men—twisted, crooked, base—we are constrained to agree with the words of an old servant of Christ. Someone objected to the words of Romans 9. 13: "Jacob have I loved, but Esau have I hated"; and when the preacher asked what was his difficulty he replied that it was occasioned by the words: "Esau have I hated." "Well, sir," replied the preacher, "how differently we are constituted. The strangest part to me is that He could have loved Jacob." And yet, as we shall see presently, out of this unpromising material God made one of the noblest of men. By the stern loving discipline of suffering, and sorrow, and loss; by unmerited grace and boundless love, the heavenly Potter transformed Jacob the supplanter—a piece of broken earthenware—into Israel a prince with God—a vessel meet for the Master's use. "Crystallized in his experience are the sorrows and struggles and weaknesses which beset the path of the majority of Christians. Every word of such a story is instinct with life, every sentence is a harbinger of hope, and our hearts sob a tribute of loving gratitude to the God of love Who has given us such a tale of matchless grace." We think of those who are daily the subjects of such grace and we say: "Happy is he that hath the God of Jacob for his help, whose hope is in the Lord his God" (Psalm 146. 5); we think of Him Who exercises the grace, and with full hearts we exclaim:

> "Glory to Him Who from the mire,
>   In patient length of days,
>   Elaborated into life
>   A people for His praise."

The record of Jacob's life is found in Genesis 25. 19-34; chapters 27 to 35; chapters 46 to 50. These portions should be carefully and repeatedly read in order that the full effects of the transformation effected in his life may be seen.

The story is in four sections: (1) From his birth to Bethel where, for the first time, he found himself consciously in the presence of God (Genesis 25. 19-34; chapters 27 and 28); (2) from Bethel to Peniel where he first surrendered to God (chapters 29 to 32); (3) from Peniel back to Bethel where he first began really to live for God (chapters 33 to 35); (4) from Bethel to Egypt, the place from which he went home to be with God (chapters 46 to 50).

From Birth to Bethel

1. BIRTHRIGHT (GENESIS 25. 29-34)

Esau was by a few minutes the elder of the two boys, and to him belonged the rights of the firstborn. The one who would receive the blessing of Isaac would be in the direct line of the Messianic promise (Genesis 12), and would inherit spiritual privileges of a very high order (Isaiah 43. 10-12; Romans 9. 4-5). But it is evident that Esau valued none of these things. In Hebrews 12. 16 he is spoken of as a "profane person who for one morsel of meat sold his birthright"; a man who for the gratification of a momentary appetite bartered eternal wealth. He preferred the present to the future, the sensual to the spiritual, sight to faith.

When we turn to Jacob we find his conduct equally reprehensible. His first recorded words are: "Sell me this day thy birthright"; and in the circumstances in which it was made, such an appeal to such a man was irresistible. While it is true that God had said that the elder would serve the younger (Genesis 25. 23) Jacob had to learn that the prophecy would be fulfilled without his scheming; that God would carry out His purposes in His Own way.

2. BLESSING (GENESIS 27)

The contents of this chapter gather round the four actors in it.

(1) ISAAC (VERSES 1-4)

There was favouritism in the home. Rebekah loved Jacob, Isaac loved Esau; and in this section we behold the aged father, who thought he was about to die, expressing his desire to bestow on his favourite what God had destined for Jacob. That desire was strongly bound up with bodily needs (verses 3-4).

(2) REBEKAH (VERSES 5-17)

Rebekah overheard what had been said and, filled with a nameless dread that the promise of God should be invalidated, she plots and schemes on behalf of her beloved Jacob. Her anxiety for the carrying out of the divine purpose was admirable; the method she adopted to ensure its being carried out was despicable. She sought a right thing in a wrong way.

(3) JACOB (VERSES 18-29)

Jacob hesitated to do as he was told, but his hesitancy was due not to the fact that it was wrong but because he feared the consequences of discovery (verses 11-12). And so he becomes a liar (verse 19), a hypocrite (verse 20), a deceiver (verse 24), and a thief (verse 35).

(4) ESAU (VERSES 30-40)

When Esau returned and found what had happened "he cried with an exceeding great and bitter cry" (verse 34 R.V.). "Those tears of Esau the bold impetuous man —almost like the cry of a trapped creature—are among the most pathetic in the Bible." "Afterward when he would have inherited the blessing he was rejected; for he found no place for repentance though he sought it carefully with tears" (Hebrews 12. 17). It should be noted, however, that he wept, not because he was a sinner, but because he was a loser; that his tears were occasioned by the evil which sin brings, and not by the sin which brought the evil. "When the New Testament tells us that he found no place for repentance, it means that there was no possibility of undoing what had been accomplished. He found no way to change his father's mind though he earnestly sought one."

We pause here to gather up some lessons: (1) "Rest in the Lord and wait patiently for Him." (2) "Good ends do not justify bad means." (3) Misery stalks in transgression's rear. (4) The firmament of God's providence overspreads the fathomless sea of His love.

3. BETHEL (GENESIS 28)

Genesis 27 ends as it began—with deceit. The enraged brother is determined to have revenge on Jacob (verse 41), and Rebekah, fearing murder, arranged for Jacob to go to her brother Laban in Mesopotamia until Esau's anger should cool (verses 42-46). Chapter 28 tells of his departure from home and of his experience at Bethel.

"A lonely wanderer, hated by his brother, and obliged to flee from home in order to save his life, Jacob learns on the very first night of his exile that he is the object of Heaven's love and care, and that the angels of God were busily passing and repassing from heaven to earth in ministering to him." In the course of his life Jacob had seven of these divine manifestations.

As he lay down to rest on that memorable night he came to one of the great crises of his life; there for the first time he came into direct touch with the living God. Despite his crooked and deceitful ways, the earnestness with which he sought the blessing proved that he was a man who valued spiritual privileges; and although God had later on to discipline him by tribulation sore, He deals with him here in tenderest grace. Three things stand out in the story:

(1) THE VISION (VERSES 10-12)

"And he dreamed and behold a ladder set up on the earth, and the top of it reached to heaven: and behold the angels of God ascending and descending on it" (verse 12). "Ascending and descending." "When we ask why this order is chosen and preserved, the answer seems to be that it lifts the veil from a divine guardianship, unthought of by us, but real and persistent. It was the relieving of the heavenly guard that Jacob witnessed. The angels of God had attended him on his way to Bethel. They were around him when he stopped, when he chose his resting place, and when he laid down his head upon the stone. They were now ascending in order that those descending might take their place." We have not realised the full significance of the fact that the people of God are the subjects of angelic ministry (2 Kings 6. 16-17; Psalm 34. 7; Daniel 6. 22; Hebrews 1. 14).

(2) THE VOICE (VERSES 13-15)

At that moment Jacob's requirements were twofold. He needed the assurance that his meanness and trickery had not robbed him of what he so earnestly craved, and this is graciously given to him (see verses 13-14). There is a phrase in verse 14 which should be noted. Abraham is the father of the earthly people as well as of all that believe, and his seed is compared to both "stars and sand" (Genesis 22. 17). Isaac is a figure of Him Who, because of His obedience unto death, will bring many sons to glory. His seed is compared to "stars" only (Genesis 26. 4). Jacob is heir of the promises according to the flesh, and his seed is compared to "dust of the earth" only (Genesis 28. 14).

But Jacob needed not only assurance regarding the glorious future; he was in distressing circumstances and required immediate comfort and help. He had just left home and was conscious of friendlessness and loneliness. This is met by Jehovah's Word: "I am with thee." He was absolutely defenceless and his heart trembled as he travels into the unknown. This is met by Jehovah's promise: "I will keep thee in all places whither thou goest." He fears that the hatred with which Esau now regarded him would forever prevent his return to the land which he was now leaving. This is met by Jehovah's assurance: "I will bring thee again into this land." Thus his loneliness is met by the assurance of divine companionship; his fearfulness, by the assurance of omnipotent protection; and his uncertainty, by the assurance of heavenly guidance.

Hazlitt sarcastically remarks that "in the days of Jacob there was a ladder between heaven and earth, but now the heavens have gone further off, and they have become astronomical." Thank God that statement is untrue, for, as Strachan has said, although the dream has faded and the symbols have vanished, and the voice is silent, the facts remain. "God is in His heaven, loving and caring for men, sending forth His ministering spirits, and Himself speaking to the souls of men. These are no mere dreams, but great realities; and the uniform result of the act of faith which accepts them is the shifting of the centre of life and all its interests from earth to heaven."

"I will not leave thee" (verse 15). That promise is repeated to the children of God again and again (Deuteronomy 31. 6; Joshua 1. 5; 1 Chronicles 28. 20; Hebrews 13. 5).

(3) THE VOW (VERSES 16-22)

Although the vision and the voice made an abiding impression on his mind, they do not seem to have vitally influenced his life. Nevertheless, although his language is faulty and his response incomplete, this first meeting with God was a thing which he never forgot (Genesis 48. 3). To commemorate it his pillow is changed into a pillar (verse 18), and he pledges himself to the service of God (verse 22).

JACOB—EXPERIENCE

From Bethel to Peniel

AFTER the thrilling experiences of the night at Bethel Jacob resumed his long journey and in due course arrived in Mesopotamia where for 20 years he was to be a pupil in the school of experience. Into the details of the story we cannot enter, but from the chapters which describe them (29 to 31) one blessed truth emerges, namely, that God weaves our web of time with mercy and with judgment. The depression of spirit occasioned by the injustice and deceit of Laban was counteracted by the presence of Rachel, the beautiful Syrian shepherdess, with whose love Jacob's life was enriched and blessed (Genesis 29. 20; Proverbs 18. 22).

At the end of 20 years of unjust treatment, the conduct of Laban became intolerable, and God providentially used this to kindle in Jacob's heart the desire to return to the land of his fathers and to his kindred (chapter 31. 3). In due course the two men separate; Laban departed and returned to his place and Jacob went on his way (Genesis 31. 55 and 32. 1). The supreme crisis of his life lay just ahead of him, and in preparation for it he becomes once more the subject of angelic ministry (Genesis 32. 1).

The command to return to his kindred recalled to Jacob's mind as vividly as if he had done it only a few hours before, the trickery by which he had defrauded Esau of his father's blessing; and the consciousness of his guilt in this connection robbed him of that confidence toward God and of that boldness toward man which characterise those who have the priceless possession of an uncondemning heart (1 John 3. 21; Proverbs 28. 1). He sent messengers to his brother, and these return with the alarming news that Esau is on his way to meet him with four hundred men (Genesis 32. 3-6). Jacob is now greatly afraid, and in his distress both plans (verses 7-8) and prays (verses 9-12). He invokes the God of his fathers at Whose command he was returning to Canaan (verse 9), confesses his unworthiness of the kindnesses which had been showered upon him (verse 10), and pleads for deliverance from the hand of his brother Esau (verses 11-12). He had little faith in the efficacy of his prayer, however, for immediately after offering it he began scheming and planning once more (verses 13-20). Apparently he was conscious that something of supreme importance was about to happen; for yielding to an overmastering desire for solitude he conducted his camp across the ford Jabbok in order that through the stillness of that memorable night he might be left alone (verses 21-24). "That night"—referred to in verses 21 and 22—he reached the turning point in his spiritual life which brought to an end for ever his trickery, cunning, and deceit, and from which he emerged a broken but a very blessed man. We shall follow the words of Scripture as we trace the stages of the conflict through which he passed.

(1) WRESTLING (VERSE 24)

"And Jacob was left alone; and there wrestled a Man with him until the breaking of the day." It should be noted that it was not Jacob who wrestled with the Man; it was the Man Who wrestled with Jacob—an entirely different thing. "This passage is often quoted as an instance of Jacob's earnestness in prayer. It is nothing of the sort. It is an instance of God's earnestness to take from us all that hinders our truest life, whilst we resist Him with all our might and main. It was not that Jacob wished to obtain aught from God, but it was that He— the angel Jehovah—had a controversy with this double-dealing and crafty child of His; desirous to break up his self-sufficiency for ever, and to give scope for the develop-

ment of the Israel that lay cramped and coffined within."
The self life is the supplanter of the Christ life, and it is
the method of our deliverance from the former that is
portrayed in the scene by Jabbok's rushing stream.

(2) CLINGING (VERSE 25)

"And when He saw that He prevailed not against him,
He touched the hollow of his thigh and the hollow of
Jacob's thigh was out of joint as He wrestled with him."
The sinew of the thigh is the strongest in the human body,
and by a touch there the mysterious Visitor rendered
Jacob helpless. The resister becomes a clinger, and learns
that the hour of his physical prostration is the hour of his
spiritual triumph. Hitherto the carnal life had dominated
him; henceforth his life was to be divinely ruled.

(3) BESEECHING (VERSE 26)

"And He said: Let me go, for the day breaketh. And
he said, I will not let Thee go except Thou bless me."
Jacob first schemed (Genesis 27), then he prayed and
schemed (Genesis 32. 9-20), but now he prays (verse 26).
"He had power over the angel and prevailed; he wept and
made supplication unto Him" (Hosea 12. 4). The supplanter becomes a supplicant, and secures by prayer and
in weakness what he could never have secured by subtlety
or strength. But before God imparts the blessing we hear
Jacob:

(4) CONFESSING (VERSE 27)

"And He said unto him: What is thy name? And he
said: Jacob." Names of old stood for character, and
before God blesses Jacob He gets from him the confession
of what he was. "You ask Me to bless you," said God.
"Very well, what is your name?" "My name is Jacob—
supplanter, deceiver, liar, hypocrite, thief; my life has

been one career of crafty cunning and vulturous greed." To that confession God immediately responds.

(5) PREVAILING (VERSE 28)

"And He said: thy name shall be called no more Jacob but Israel; for as a prince hast thou power with God and with men, and hast prevailed." "The new name expresses the result of that night's struggle. Jacob the self-willed supplanter who insisted on having his own way becomes submissive to the divine rule. He who had striven against God is at last conquered and joyfully acknowledges himself vassal of the divine conqueror." This is indeed the victory of surrender. Up till now his life in the main was one of subtlety and trickery; from this night on his life in the main was one of simplicity and trust.

It is interesting to notice how God adapts His dealings with His people to their individual requirements. Jacob was broken before he received the blessing; Paul was broken after it (compare Genesis 32; 2 Corinthians 12). The one was crippled in order that he might be crowned; the other was humbled lest he should be exalted.

(6) ENQUIRING (VERSE 29)

"And Jacob asked Him and said: tell me, I pray thee, Thy name. And He said: wherefore is it that thou dost ask after My name?" As names in Scripture are expressive of character, Jacob's request was really one for fuller knowledge of the Person to Whom he was now clinging. The reply which he gets resembles the reply which Moses received when he made a similar request (Exodus 3. 13-14). That name was to remain undisclosed until the coming of the Lord Jesus, Who, as the end of His earthly life was approaching, could say: "I have manifested Thy name unto the men whom Thou gavest Me out of the world" (John 17. 6). But although God could not fully reveal Himself to Jacob, "He blessed him there" (Psalm 20. 1).

(7) BEHOLDING (VERSE 30)

"And Jacob called the name of the place Peniel; for I have seen God face to face and my life is preserved." The thought enshrined in these words is that of privilege or favour (Deuteronomy 34. 10)—it is the beatific vision. Moses enjoyed this privilege (Exodus 33. 11); David earnestly sought it (Psalm 27. 4); we may daily possess it. "We all with unveiled face beholding as in a mirror the glory of the Lord are transformed into the same image from glory to glory even as by the Spirit of the Lord" (2 Corinthians 3. 18).

> "The soul whose sight all quickening grace renews,
> Takes the resemblance of the One she views,
> As diamonds stripped of their opaque disguise,
> Reflect the noontide glory of the skies."

"And He blessed him there" (*verse* 29)

"Where? (1) In the place of loneliness where he was alone with God (verse 24); (2) in the place of weakness where the sinew shrank (verse 25); (3) in the place of supplication where he wept and prayed (verse 26; Hosea 12. 4); (4) in the place of confession where he admitted his guilt (verse 27); (5) in the place of power where a princely walk began (verse 28); (6) in the place of enquiry where a deeper knowledge of God was sought (verse 29); (7) in the place of vision where he saw the face of God (verse 30).

Midnight; Daybreak; Sunshine

There are three points of time referred to in Genesis 32, and these emblemise the ordeal through which Jacob passed, the victory which he achieved, and the results which followed. There was midnight conflict—protracted and severe (verses 21-22); daybreak blessing—complete and permanent (verse 26); midday sunshine—without and within (verse 31). From the last named hour there is no trace of anything in Jacob but princeliness of conduct and nobleness of life. He emerged from the crisis a changed man.

From Peniel back to Bethel

1. THE MEETING WITH ESAU (CHAPTER 33)

The finest exposition of this chapter is a verse in the book of Proverbs (chapter 16. 7): "When a man's ways please the Lord He maketh even his enemies to be at peace with him." "He who meets God at dawn will not fear to meet man at noon."

Both Esau and Jacob say: "I have enough" (verses 9 and 11); but whereas the former merely states the fact, the latter attributes his satisfaction to the grace of God.

2. THE STAY AT SHECHEM (CHAPTER 34)

It would seem that on his arrival at Shechem, Jacob temporarily abandoned the pilgrim character; we now read for the first time of one of the patriarchs building a house (chapter 33. 17). The sequel proves, too, that in Jacob's household there had been compromise with the idolators among whom they dwelt (chapter 35. 2). He had to pay a terrible price for these things, for his daughter was dishonoured (chapter 34. 2), and his sons, who avenged the wrong done to their sister, were guilty of barbarous injustice and cruelty (verses 6-31).

3. THE RETURN TO BETHEL

"If Genesis 34 is godless, Genesis 35 is full of God. The former describes the Shechem life of the Hebrews; the latter, their Bethel life. The contrast between a believer's and an unbeliever's life is scarcely more marked than the contrast between a half-hearted and a whole-hearted believer's life."

In the midst of the sorrow and terror occasioned by the happenings recorded in Genesis 34, God appeared "and said unto Jacob: arise, go up to Bethel and dwell there" (Genesis 35. 1). It was a spiritual as well as a physical ascent, and it necessitated drastic reformations in the home (35. 2). These, however, were duly effected, and God's servant reached once more the place where God met him for the first time. Here, recalled to "his first love" (Revelation 2. 4) he began really to live for God.

RACHEL

A man who walks with God is not necessarily exempted from trial, for in this chapter we have the story of the death of Rachel, the only woman whom Jacob ever really loved. The story of her death, says Strachan, "is the tale of an agony too deep for passion, or tears, or earthly remedy. There are only five verses (Genesis 35. 16-20) and they contain but a bare record of facts; yet this is one of the most beautifully touching passages in sacred writ. Jacob's love for Rachel began with tears of joy at the well of Haran. When she is so suddenly snatched from him by the hand of death, the springs of his emotion seem to be dried up. His sorrow was too deep for tears. His wound never healed. Long after, when he was lying far from his native land in his gilded Egyptian chamber awaiting his own end, he recalled that journey to Ephrath—the halt by the way, the agonised suspense, the last words, the awful stillness—and with touching simplicity he said: "She died to my sorrow" (Genesis 48. 7 R.V.m.).

"The tomb of Jacob's earthly hopes was, however, the birthplace of his heavenly ones. Ephrath and Bethlehem were one and the same place" (Genesis 48. 7; Matthew 2. 6).

From Bethel to Egypt

From Genesis 37 the story of Jacob's life becomes inextricably bound up with the lives of his sons; and, of the sons, Joseph is the one who stands out prominently in the records from chapters 37 to 45. At chapter 46

Jacob again comes before us and remains so till almost the close of the book.

It is interesting to note that the first seventeen years of Joseph's life were spent in Canaan with his father Jacob, and that the last seventeen years of Jacob's life were spent in Egypt with his son Joseph (compare Genesis 37. 2; 47. 28).

1. PHARAOH

In response to Joseph's request (45. 13), and with divine permission (46. 3-4), Jacob went down to Egypt, and was introduced to the greatest monarch of his age. When in the presence of the king Jacob bestowed on him his blessing (47. 10); and without all contradiction the less is blessed of the better. For while Pharaoh was heir to the throne of Egypt, Jacob was heir of the promises of God.

2. TESTIMONY

In Genesis 48. 15-16 we have Jacob's final testimony to the goodness and grace of God. He speaks of God as "the One before Whom his fathers walked—the God of history; as the God Who had shepherded him all his life long—the God of providence; and as the Angel Who had redeemed him from all evil—the God of grace." Faithfulness is linked with the first of these titles, sustenance with the second, and redemption with the third.

3. DEATH

The life of Jacob had been a stormy one, but as the years passed over his head the clouds disappeared and his closing days resembled the setting of a summer sun which is brightest just before it disappears.

As the hour of his dissolution approached he faced it calmly and manfully. He quietly yielded up his spirit to the God Who gave it and was gathered unto his people (chapter 49. 33).

CHAPTER TWENTY-TWO

JOSEPH—THE VICTORIOUS

(Genesis 37 and 39 to 50)

WE now reach the last of the seven outstanding men of Genesis, and the fourth in the history of the chosen race. Joseph is an almost flawless character, and forms the ideal type of redeemed and sanctified manhood. He possesses in pre-eminent degree the virtues of his ancestors, but is devoid of the faults which occasionally marred their lives. His faith in God is similar to that of Abraham, but is more constant; his acquiescence in the will of God is as pronounced as that of Isaac, but is much more intelligent; he has the ability of Jacob without his cunning. Both the active and the passive virtues are seen in him in balanced perfection. He knew how to take occasion by the hand; and he knew how to rest in the Lord and wait patiently for Him. His life abounds with incidents which set forth his noble character; with happenings which throw light on the deepest of life's mysteries; with experiences which illustrate some of the great principles by which the servants of God are trained for wider usefulness. For the present we confine ourselves to an examination of the Scriptures which reveal

Joseph—the man

"Men like Joseph," says Gelesnoff, "are rare visitors among mortals. As a comet, set like a gem in nocturnal blue, silvers her way in the sky, drawing universal attention and admiration, and then vanishes as suddenly as it came, not to reappear again for hundreds of years, so men of Joseph's calibre are few and far apart in the history of the race." We shall now proceed to examine nine of the lovely traits by which his character was distinguished;

and if, as we do so, we are made conscious of shortcoming, let us remind ourselves that the power by means of which Joseph triumphed long ago is unreservedly at our disposal to-day (Genesis 41. 38; Ephesians 5. 18).

(1) HE WAS TRUSTFUL

By that I mean that his faith in God was childlike and unwavering. Again and again in the course of the narrative this fact stands out as the supreme factor in his life. It delivered him from the most powerful temptation to which a young man can be exposed (chapter 39. 9); and it enabled him, after the stern experiences through which he passed as an exile, a slave, and a felon, to recognise the hand and the goodness of God in it all (chapter 45. 5).

There is a profound lesson for us here. It may be that your heart is tortured by sorrows which are too sad for utterance and too deep for tears; that your mind is perplexed by dark enigmas of permitted wrong; that your body is racked with almost ceaseless pain, and that in the presence of these problems your faith is so weak that you are ready to cry out with Jacob: "All these things are against me" (chapter 42. 36). But it is not really so. Our Lord Jesus assures us that there is a special providence in the fall of a sparrow, and that we are of more value than many sparrows (Luke 12. 7). He tells us, what Joseph ultimately proved, that all things work together for good to them that love God (Genesis 50. 20; Romans 8. 28); and the acceptance as literally true, of this Word from our God, will give central peace at the heart of our stormswept lives.

> "If our faith were but more simple,
>   We would take Him at His Word,
> And our lives would be all gladness
>   In the sunshine of our Lord."

(2) HE WAS HUMBLE

After the recital of his dream, the king said to Joseph: "I have heard say of thee that thou canst understand a dream to interpret it" (chapter 41. 15). But the noble youth immediately disclaimed all merit and said: "It is not in me: God shall give Pharaoh an answer of peace" (verse 16).

"It is not in me." Those who have measured themselves in the presence of God are well aware of that fact. They know that they have nothing which they did not receive (1 Corinthians 4. 7), and consequently the language of their hearts ever is: "Not unto us, O Lord, not unto us, but unto Thy Name give glory" (Psalm 115. 1).

> "How baseless is the mightiest earthly pride,
> The diamond is but charcoal purified;
> The loveliest pearl that decks a monarch's breast
> Is but an insect's sepulchre at best."

(3) HE WAS TRUSTWORTHY

In the house of the Egyptian official (chapter 39. 6), in the prison (chapter 39. 22-23), and ultimately as premier of Egypt (chapter 41. 55), Joseph was a trusted man. Each of his masters relied on him with such absolute confidence that what is said of one of them is true of them all. "He left all that he had in Joseph's hand; and he knew not aught he had, save the bread which he did eat" (Genesis 39. 6).

This is a trait which every Christian man should earnestly seek to exemplify. Whether in great things or in small his word should be his bond. The wise king expresses what many have felt and proved, namely, that "confidence in an unfaithful man in time of trouble is like a broken tooth, and a foot out of joint" (Proverbs 25. 19). Apparently in his time faithful men were rare (Proverbs 20. 6).

(4) HE WAS PURE

It is scarcely possible to imagine a more terrific temptation for a young man of Joseph's age than that which is described in Genesis 39. 7-10. Its appeal was twofold; it offered the opportunity for the gratification of passion; and it held out a short cut to high promotion—appetite and ambition. Joseph was no glorified saint, he was a man of like passions with ourselves, but in the name and strength of God he put the sin away. He refused (Genesis 39. 8), and was enabled to do so by his loyalty to his master (verse 8) and his faithfulness to God (verse 9). "How can I do this great wickedness and sin against God?" We read nothing all through Joseph's life of his inner spiritual experience. But this one sentence, spoken in the hour of temptation, is eloquent to tell us what it must have been. He must have walked with God in close and watchful intercourse.

The lesson which this incident teaches remains for all time. Some temptations are more effectively mastered by flight than by conflict, and the temptation to impurity is one of them (Proverbs 7; 2 Timothy 2. 22).

(5) HE WAS PROSPEROUS

His prosperity was due to the companionship of God. "The Lord was with Joseph and he was a prosperous man" (Genesis 39. 2). Strange that this should be said of a man who was a slave in a palace (verse 2), and repeated of him when he was cast into a dungeon (verse 23). It clearly proves that,

"Stone walls do not a prison make, nor iron bars a cage."

"The oppressor held his body bound, but knew not what a range his spirit took, unconscious of a chain; and that to bind him is a vain attempt, whom God delights in and in whom He dwells." In the estimation of the worldling, Joseph's prosperity only began when he was raised to be the second man in the Egyptian empire; in actual fact he prospered in slavery and imprisonment.

In the New Testament soul-prosperity is regarded as the secret and criterion of all true prosperity (3 John 2).

(6) He was adaptable

"It is easy to see, if we read between the lines, that speaking after the manner of men, his adaptability was a potent factor in his success. He did not struggle against a higher might; he bowed to the inevitable and adjusted himself to it. He had learned that acquiescence in affliction is the first step in the way out of it, and was thus ready to enter the doors which God flung open at the critical turnings of his history. If he had violently withstood his brothers they would have killed him, but his docile deportment won him the sympathies of Reuben, who dissuaded the others from their murderous intent. If he had not cheerfully served the interests of Potiphar, the latter would have executed him on the strength of his wife's accusation. If he had been brooding over his miseries in the dungeon, he would have missed the opportunity of interpreting the dream to the chief butler—an event which paved the way for his ultimate elevation to the second place in the kingdom."

The ability to accommodate oneself to any new environment, in which the providence of God may place one, is a thing of great value. Making the best of circumstances is the art of living. To regard these circumstances as an opportunity for the service of God is the secret of abounding joy.

(7) He was brave

To people who boasted of their self-sufficiency he testified of the true God. He did this in two ways: (1) By life—"His master saw that the Lord was with him" (chapter 39. 3). (2) By lip. To this heathen king he was not afraid to speak of the living God (chapter 41. 25). The people saw that the Lord was with him, before they heard him say that He was with him.

These two things—what we are and what we say—remain to this day the channels of testimony for God.

(8) HE WAS WISE

It is stated that God gave him wisdom (Acts 7. 9-10) and that Pharaoh recognised this (Genesis 41. 38-39). The work with which he was entrusted "required a vast organising, farseeing genius, and he proved equal to the task. He won the eulogies which are bestowed on a great ruler, by a grateful nation. 'Thou hast saved our lives,' they said; and when they bowed the knee to him it was not the mechanical homage of servile fear, but the sincere reverence of whole-hearted gratitude."

Wisdom to conduct ourselves in the affairs of life is promised to those who truly ask for it (James 1. 5-6). These verses answer three questions: What to ask—Wisdom; Whom to ask—God; How to ask—In faith.

(9) HE WAS AFFECTIONATE

The pathetic scene described in Genesis 50. 15-21 reveals the tenderness of his heart. His brethren were afraid that, after the death of their father, Joseph would wreak his vengeance on them, "and they sent a messenger unto Joseph, saying: thy father did command before he died, saying: so shall ye say unto Joseph, Forgive, I pray thee now, the trespass of thy brethren, and their sin; for they did unto thee evil; and now, we pray thee, forgive the trespass of the servants of the God of thy father" (verses 16-17). He listened to the message with a sorrowful heart. "It was a sad disappointment to his sunny and generous nature that he was so greatly misunderstood. Yet their suspicions only serve to display the generous sympathy of his nature. As he realises what they have been suffering he cannot keep back his tears. 'Joseph wept when they spake unto him.' The strongest quality in Joseph's character is forgiving love. We see in him the personification of healing mercy and redeeming grace. It is the Christian spirit before the Christian time."

Two considerations will enable us to act as Joseph

acted when we are wronged by our fellow-men. The first is that God overrules everything for His people's good (verse 20); and the second, the apprehension of the matchless grace that has been extended to ourselves. "Be ye kind one to another, tender hearted, forgiving one another, even as God for Christ's sake hath forgiven you" (Ephesians 4. 32).

The Providence of God

"It is deeply instructive to trace the hand of God in every step of Joseph's path, from the days of his youth when feeding the flock in Canaan, to the day of his glory when set over all the land of Egypt. The varied characters that crossed his path—the father that loved him, the brethren that hated him, the merchants that carried him to Egypt, the captain that promoted him, the woman that traduced him, the jailor that showed him favour, the butler by whom he was forgotten, and the king by whom he was exalted—all were the unconscious instruments to carry out God's purpose for him."

The tracing of the winding thread of providential arrangement in our lives will be of great service to us as we face the trials by which they are beset. Indeed, without the assurance that we are under the loving care of One Who is infinitely wise we would despair.

"One adequate support for the calamities of mortal life
    Exists: one only—an assured belief
    That the procession of our fate, howe'er
    Sad or disturbed, is ordered by a Being
    Of infinite benevolence and power,
    Whose everlasting purposes embrace
    All accidents, converting them to good."

Believe that, then trust in God and do the right.

Lessons from Joseph's life

(1)   Whom the Lord loveth He chasteneth (Hebrews 12. 6).

(2) Blessed are the pure in heart: for they shall see God (Matthew 5. 8).

(3) When thou passest through the waters, I will be with thee (Isaiah 43. 2).

(4) Fret not: He shall bring forth thy righteousness as the light (Psalm 37. 1, 6).

(5) All things work together for good to them that love God (Romans 8. 28).

(6) If any man have a quarrel against any, even as Christ forgave you, so also do ye (Colossians 3. 13).

(7) Chastening . . . afterward yieldeth the peaceable fruit of righteousness unto them which are exercised thereby (Hebrews 12. 11).

(8) Rest in the Lord, and wait patiently for Him (Psalm 37. 7).

CHAPTER TWENTY-THREE

JOSEPH—THE SERVANT OF GOD

FROM the Scriptures which describe the outstanding characteristics of the life of Joseph we learn that "the conflicts which he had to wage, unlike those of his predecessor, were all external. There was little in him of that antagonism between flesh and spirit, that alternation between good and evil, strength and weakness, which preponderated in Jacob. From the very first he heartily embraced the truth; and his struggles were not so much with himself in order to maintain individual allegiance as they were with others who impeded its advance." Let us now follow the steps by which, in spite of these external hindrances, he was led from obscurity and infamy to triumph and fame.

A careful reading of the records shows that his life is in two great divisions. The first of these is detailed in Genesis chapter 37 and chapters 39 to 41. 13, and may be summed up in one word—humiliation. The second is contained in chapter 41. 14 to chapter 50 and it, too, may be summed up in one word—exaltation. In the first half we see Joseph being trained and fitted for the position which he was ultimately to occupy, and for the carrying out of the purposes of God; in the second, we see him discharging the duties which devolved upon him as a ruler and administrator, and as the necessary link between Israel as a family and Israel as a nation. The one teaches that before honour is humility (Proverbs 18. 12); the other, that he that humbleth himself shall be exalted (Luke 14. 11).

1. EQUIPPED AND PREPARED (CHAPTER 37 AND CHAPTER 39 TO 41. 13)

These Scriptures set forth the usual method by which

God prepares those whom He would greatly use or richly bless. Just as it is by fire that gold is separated from its dross, and iron is hardened into steel, so it is in the furnace of affliction that the moral equivalents of these things are produced in the lives of the servants of God.

The process through which Joseph was allowed to pass was threefold; and the first of these was

(a) Exile

Loyalty to vision led to banishment from home (Genesis 37). As the sequel proved, the narration of his dream by Joseph was not occasioned by any sense of his superiority to his brothers but by a premonition from God of the destiny which awaited him. That narration, however, cost him dear for, incensed by it they sought to kill him, and were restrained from doing so only by the thought that banishment from home and kindred would equally prevent the fulfilment of the dreams. "Moved with envy they sold Joseph into Egypt" (Acts 7. 9). Here began the afflictions of Joseph—those grindings on the wheel which made him a vessel chaste and beautiful, meet for the Master's use (Acts 7. 10).

(b) Slavery

The change from first place in his father's affection to exposure for sale on an Egyptian slave market must have been a terrible one. But there is no indication that his heart became embittered; indeed, the evidence is all the other way. He served his new master so whole-heartedly that he became Potiphar's most trusted servant, when suddenly, for the second time, his life went all to pieces. On the gravest charge, short of murder, which can be brought against any man, he passed to the final stage of his humiliation, namely,

(c) Imprisonment

"Joseph's master took him and put him into the prison, a place where the king's prisoners were bound: and he was there in the prison" (Genesis 39. 20). They hurt his feet with fetters; he was laid in iron (Psalm 105. 18).

"All through this section we are conscious of a duplex current. God works for Joseph; an unknown and unnamed power, operating through human instruments, works against him. The two movements run side by side, each leading up to a definite climax." Thus, although everything seemed against him, Scripture tells us that God was with him whether in exile (Acts 7. 9), in slavery (Genesis 39. 1-2), or in imprisonment (Genesis 39. 20-21).

The cumulative effect of these experiences—the iniquity of his brethren, the injustice of Potiphar, the ingratitude of the butler—taught him to cease from man whose breath is in his nostrils, and to place himself unreservedly in the hands of God.

2. COMMISSIONED AND BLESSED (CHAPTER 41. 14 TO CHAPTER 50)

Joseph has now reached a point in humiliation beyond which it is impossible to descend, but in it all he retained that quiet dignity which made him stand out as a prince among men, and as a witness for God. He has been (1) tested in adversity (chapter 37; chapters 39 and 40); he has been (2) tempted to impurity (chapter 39. 7-12); and because he emerged from these trials scatheless and triumphant he is now to be (3) trusted with prosperity (chapters 41 to 50).

In what has been called the highest ethical watermark in the Old Testament we are told that the Lord requires of His servants to do justly, to love mercy, and to walk humbly with their God (Micah 6. 8); and these were perhaps the outstanding lessons which Joseph learned in the hard school in which he graduated. He had been treated with rank injustice, but as a ruler would ever remember to do justly; he suffered much cruelty, but in his treatment of the wrong-doers it is quite evident that he learned to love mercy; he learned his inability to do any

thing as of himself (chapter 41. 16), and so walked humbly
with his God. He is therefore ready to be entrusted
with almost supreme power; and the chapters before us
now show that just as his humiliation had not embittered
his heart, so his exaltation did not turn his head.

Into the details of his rise to power we shall not enter,
further than to say that he became under God the preser-
ver of the human race in a time of almost world-wide
calamity. He guided a great people through years of
abundance and of want until the danger was passed and
Egypt was saved. It is a most interesting fact that
recent discoveries by Egyptologists record the fact of this
seven years' famine, and that the dates given correspond
exactly with accepted Bible chronology.

(a) The purpose of God

There is, however, a matter to which I would call special
attention and that is, the marvellous workings of the
providence of God in the development of His purposes with
the chosen race. God had sent Joseph into Egypt before
his kindred in order that he might preserve their lives by
a great deliverance (chapter 45. 7); but there was a wider
purpose than that in his going. In Canaan they were
merely a family, and as such were too insignificant in
numbers to arouse the suspicion of the Canaanites among
whom they dwelt. But any signs of great numerical
increase on their part would immediately bring them into
conflict with these peoples, and the problem was "how
should they ever get past the critical point in their history
at which they would be strong enough to excite the
jealousy and hatred of the native tribes, and yet not strong
enough to defend themselves.

The solution of that problem was supplied by God
Himself. He sent Joseph before them and gave him
favour with the Egyptian king (Psalm 105. 17; Acts 7.
10); He used Jacob's affection for Joseph to bring him
and his family down to Egypt (Genesis 45. 28); He

moved Pharaoh to give Joseph's people a dwelling-place in one of the choicest portions of the land (47. 5-6); He used the prejudices of the Egyptians to so place His people that they would be in Egypt and yet not of it (46. 31-34); and He kept them there until they became stronger than their enemies (Psalm 105. 23-24). Thus was fulfilled the word which God spake to Jacob: "Fear not to go down into Egypt; for I will *there* make of thee a great nation" (chapter 46. 3).

"His purposes will ripen fast, unfolding every hour."

(b) Treatment of his brethren

In his treatment of his brethren, described in chapters 42 to 45, we have evidence of the divine wisdom with which God had endowed him. The days of his humiliation are at an end, he is now in possession of imperial supremacy, and his brethren come under his power. How shall he deal with them?

If he were to deal with them righteously he would consign them to their merited doom. If he were to deal with them sentimentally, he would say nothing about the past, and let bygones be bygones. But if he is to deal with them graciously, then all must be brought to the light and fully confessed. For true grace reigns through righteousness and not at the expense of it; and a matter of this sort could never really be settled, until it was settled aright.

The skill by which he led them on to confession of their sin against him, and a sense of its blackness in the sight of God is very wonderful. "Had he thought of his own dignity, and his own affection, he would have revealed himself at once to his brothers. Such a revelation would have produced confusion but not repentance. He loved them, and therefore sought their spiritual welfare. He acted so as to bring the sin to their remembrance, and to make them confess it with their own lips. His plan succeeded admirably; his sternness and his kindness both conspired to disquiet them, and his goodness helped to lead them to repentance."

(c) Closing scenes

Omitting much that is absorbingly interesting we pass to the closing scenes. Joseph clearly recognised that he was raised up for purposes greater even than the saving of an empire from famine, and in chapter 50. 24 we see him turning from the earthly glory which that great work had brought him, and speaking of the things which lay nearest his heart. "Joseph said unto his brethren: I die; and God will surely visit you, and bring you out of this land unto the land which He sware to Abraham, to Isaac, and to Jacob." These words speak of the frailty of man, the faithfulness of God, the power of God, and the land of God. Joseph's faith looked *back* and he saw that the whole of his rugged pathway was paved with love (50. 20); it looked *on* and he anticipated the complete and final fulfilment of the purposes of God (50. 24).

"And Joseph took an oath of the children of Israel saying, God will surely visit you, and ye shall carry up my bones from hence" (verse 25). That command was eventually carried out (Exodus 13. 19; Joshua 24. 32).

"So Joseph died . . . and he was put in a coffin in Egypt" (50. 26). How true, so far as earth is concerned, are the poet's words:

> "The boast of heraldry, the pomp of power,
> And all that beauty, all that wealth e'er gave,
> Await alike the inevitable hour,
> The paths of glory lead but to the grave."

But this is only the end of Genesis—that is, the end of the beginning. "Turn the leaf: Exodus; Joshua; Kings; Christ. We do our little work and cease, as the coral insects which perish by myriads on the rising reef; but God's work goes on, His temple rises age after age."

Chapter Twenty-Four

CHRIST IN GENESIS

THE title of this chapter may sound strange to some, but will be perfectly intelligible to those who have read the Scriptures with Spirit-enlightened eyes. For on three occasions the Lord Jesus clearly indicates that Moses wrote of Him (Luke 24. 27 and 44; John 5. 46); and Paul affirms that Adam was a figure or type of Christ, and that Melchisedek was made like unto the Son of God (Romans 5. 14; Hebrews 7. 1-3).

"Moses wrote of Me." There is a gospel according to Moses, then, as well as according to Matthew, and Mark, and Luke, and John; and I am persuaded that the study of the typology of the Pentateuch will not only shatter all the modern theories of the composition and authorship of these divine writings, but will also unveil Christ to our hearts, giving us deep insight into the mystery of His sacred Person, and clearer apprehensions of the value of His finished work. Here, indeed, we find

> "Deep shadows of the spear-pierced side
> And thorn encompassed Head."

Speaking broadly there are three classes of types: (1) Historical; of which Israel's journeyings from Egypt to Canaan are an illustration (1 Corinthians 10. 11 margin); (2) Institutional; of which the Passover is an illustration (1 Corinthians 5. 7); and (3) Personal; of which we give you three illustrations from the book of Genesis—Melchisedek; Isaac; Joseph. While it is true that we have divine authority for speaking of only the first of these three men as directly typical of Christ, the analogies which exist between the experiences of the other two and those of our Lord are too striking and too numerous to be accidental.

(1) MELCHISEDEK

Melchisedek was a type of Christ because of the dignity of his person, because of the permanency of his priesthood, and because he held the sceptre as well as the censer—he was a king as well as a priest.

(a) *The dignity of his person (Hebrews 7. 4)*

"Consider how great this man was." The point before us now shows that the silences of Scripture are as much inspired as are its utterances; for it is partly because of the things that are not recorded of Melchisedek that he is a type of Christ. He was "without father or mother, having neither beginning of days nor end of life"—that is to say, there is no mention of his ancestors or descendants, no trace of his birth or of his death (Hebrews 7. 3). For this reason he foreshadows One Who is eternal; he "is made like unto the Son of God" (verse 3).

Not only so. Although the sons of Levi were in such a position of supremacy over the other tribes of Israel that they had "a commandment to take tithes of the people according to the law" (verse 5), the superiority of Melchisedek is manifested by the fact that he received tithes from Abraham—the progenitor of Levi—and gave Abraham his blessing (Hebrews 7. 5-10; Genesis 14. 18-20). "And without all contradiction the less is blessed of the better."

And yet great as this man was, he was only a figure of One Who was infinitely greater (Hebrews 7. 21-22).

(b) *The permanency of his priesthood*

Of the Aaronic priests it is written that they "were not suffered to continue by reason of death" (Hebrews 7. 23) —which means that they received the priesthood from their predecessors, and in due course it passed to their successors. The priesthood of Melchisedek, on the other hand, was neither derived nor transmitted; and in this respect also he symbolises Christ of Whom it is written: "Thou art a priest forever, after the order of Melchisedek" (Hebrews 7. 21).

Upon the last named fact is based one of the most heartening statements to be found in the whole of the book of God. "Wherefore He is able also to save them to the uttermost that come unto God by Him, seeing He ever liveth to make intercession for them" (verse 25). He is alive in the power of an endless life, intercedes unceasingly on behalf of His people, and is, in consequence, able to save to the uttermost of their need, and to the end of time (see also Jude 24; 2 Corinthians 9. 8; Ephesians 3. 20).

"There Thou art interceding for all who on Thee rest,
And many hearts are learning to lean upon Thy breast,
Till Thou shalt come in glory Thy ransomed saints to raise,
To chant the joyful story in songs of loudest praise."

(c) Priest and King

Melchisedek was king of Salem and priest of the most high God (Hebrews 7. 1). He was the only person in the Old Testament who held two such offices. King Uzziah attempted to usurp this prerogative and had to pay dearly for doing so (see 2 Chronicles 26. 16-21).

Our Lord Jesus did not belong to the priestly tribe "for it is evident that our Lord sprang out of Judah—the royal tribe; of which tribe Moses spake nothing concerning priesthood" (Hebrews 7. 14). It is for this reason that while on earth even He would not claim privileges which belonged exclusively to the tribe of Levi (Hebrews 8. 4). But, wondrous thought, we have now "an High Priest Who is set on the right hand of the throne of the Majesty in the heavens" (Hebrews 8. 1)—there is once more the union of royal and sacerdotal prerogatives.

It should be noted that Scripture distinguishes between Christ's throne and the Father's throne. The Lord Jesus is now seated on the latter (Revelation 3. 21); but by-and-by He shall sit and rule upon His own throne and when He does so "He shall be a priest upon His throne" (Zechariah 6. 13).

(2) ISAAC

Each of the five books of Moses has a chapter which sets forth some aspect of what the gospel of redeeming grace secures for guilty man. Thus in Genesis 22 the great truth is Substitution; in Exodus 12, Redemption; in Leviticus 16, Atonement; in Numbers 19, Cleansing; and in Deuteronomy 19, Security.

Here, however, we are to look at Genesis 22 from the point of view in which Isaac appears as a picture of Christ. He does so in four particulars: In his willing obedience; in his being offered as a sacrifice; in his figurative restoration from the dead; and in the reward which followed his obedience.

Before we turn to these matters it should be noted: (1) that when Abraham responded to the divine command: "Take now thine only son Isaac whom thou lovest and get thee into the land of Moriah and offer him there for a burnt-offering," he "entered into fellowship with God concerning the sufferings of the Holy One; that his heart vibrated—in small measure—with the same feeling which agitated the heart of God when He gave His Son to die for us"; (2) that the unconscious prophecy which Abraham uttered in verse 8: "God will provide Himself a lamb for a burnt-offering," found its deepest fulfilment in John 1. 29: "Behold the Lamb of God which taketh away the sin of the world"; and (3) that just as Abraham and Isaac were alone upon the mountains of Moriah (verse 5), so God and Christ were alone amid the solitudes of Calvary.

(a) Obedience

Although Isaac had reached an age at which it would have been possible for him to resist his father, he acquiesced unquestioningly, "and they went both of them together. And they came to the place which God had told him of; and Abraham built an altar there, and laid the wood in order, and bound Isaac his son, and laid him on the altar upon the wood" (verses 8-9). Isaac was thus worthy of his father's love. All the most beautiful traits of filial devotion are seen in his character—responsiveness to strong and tender love, recognition of the claims of age and wisdom, openness of mind and wondering eagerness to learn, and obedience unto death.

To find another instance of a Son voluntarily surrendering His life and laying Himself upon the altar at a Father's bidding, we have to go from Moriah to Calvary. It is true that God so loved the world that He gave His only begotten Son; it is equally true that Christ Jesus came into the world to save sinners; that He delighted to do His Father's will; that He became obedient unto death. "Therefore doth My Father love Me because I lay down My life that I might take it again. No man taketh it from Me, but I lay it down of Myself . . . this commandment have I received from My Father" (John 10. 17-18). These verses show us that, in the reconciliation of a doomed world, "they went both of them together" (2 Corinthians 5. 19).

(b) Sacrifice

"And Abraham stretched forth his hand, and took the knife to slay his son" (verse 10).

It is evident both from Genesis 22 and Hebrews 11 that Abraham had in the purpose of his heart gone to such full lengths with God that God credits him with having done what He commanded him to do. "Because thou hast done this thing, and hast not withheld thy son, thine only son . . . in blessing I will bless thee" (Genesis 22. 16-17). "By faith Abraham when he was tried offered up Isaac" (Hebrews 11. 17). At the critical moment, however, a messenger of God arrested the uplifted arm; Abraham's parental feelings and Isaac's precious life were spared.

Passing to what is foreshadowed in all this we learn that while God spared Abraham's son "He spared not His own Son but delivered Him up for us all" (Romans 8. 32).

> "Jehovah bade His sword awake, O Christ it woke
>   'gainst Thee;
> Thy blood the flaming blade must slake. Thy heart
>   its sheath must be
> All for my sake, my peace to make,
>   Now sleeps that sword for me.

(c) Restoration

It has been said that when Abraham stated to the young men: "I and the lad will go yonder, and worship, and come again to you" (verse 5), he deceived them. But that was by no means so. His promise that they would both return evidences the marvellous nature of his faith in God. He was convinced that if Isaac's life were taken, God would raise him again from the dead, "accounting that God was able to raise him up even from the dead; from whence also he received him in a figure" (Hebrews 11. 19).

The Lord Jesus Who actually entered the domain of death rose a conqueror over the tomb; and His word to the seer of Patmos was: "I am He that liveth, and was dead; and behold I am alive for evermore" (Revelation 1. 18).

(d) Reward

Language seems incapable of expressing what God thought of Abraham because of his unreserved surrender; and among the blessings which became his because of it, was the promise of an innumerable seed (Genesis 22. 17) —a promise that was afterwards repeated to Isaac (chapter 26. 4).

Turning once more to our blessed Lord we learn that consequent on His obedience unto death, He is the Head of a redeemed race—a multitude which no man can number. "He shall see his seed . . . He shall see of the travail of His soul, and shall be satisfied" (Isaiah 53. 10-11).

(3) JOSEPH

Joseph: *Christ:*
Humiliation.   *Suffering.*

Gen. 37. 3.	(a) Beloved by his father.	Matt. 3. 17.
Acts 7. 9.	(b) Envied by his brethren.	Mark 15. 10.
Gen. 37. 20.	(c) Rejected by his brethren.	John 1. 11.
Gen. 37. 28.	(d) Sold for silver.	Matt. 26. 15.

Exaltation.   *Glory.*

Gen. 41. 42-43.	(a) Exalted to pre-eminence	Phil. 2. 9.
Gen. 41. 57.	(b) Meeting the world's deep hunger.	John 6. 51.
Gen. 41. 45.	(c) Marrying a Gentile bride.	Acts 15. 14.
Acts 7. 13.	(d) Revealing himself to his brethren.	Zech. 12. 10.

Christ and Genesis 3

The following helpful words remind our hearts afresh what we owe to our matchless, glorious Saviour, and thus form a fitting and worthy conclusion to our meditations on the book of Genesis:

"We turn now to contemplate Christ Himself bearing the curse of the Fall. What was the punishment which followed the first Adam's sin? In answering this question we confine ourselves to the chapter now before us. Beginning at the seventeenth verse of Genesis 3, we may trace a sevenfold consequence upon the entrance of sin into this world. First, the ground was cursed. Second, in sorrow man was to eat of it all the days of his life. Third, thorns and thistles it was to bring forth. Fourth, in the sweat of his face man was to eat his bread. Fifth, unto dust man was to return. Sixth, a flaming sword barred his way to the tree of life. Seventh, there was the execution of God's warning that in the day man partook of the forbidden fruit he should surely die. Such was the doom which fell upon Adam as the result of the Fall.

Observe now how completely the Lord Jesus bore the full consequences of man's sin. First, Christ was "made a curse for us" (Galatians 3. 13). Second, so thoroughly was He acquainted with grief, He was denominated "the man of sorrows" (Isaiah 53. 3). Third, in order that we might know how literally the Holy One bore in His own body the consequences of Adam's sin, we read "Then came Jesus forth wearing the crown of thorns" (John 19. 5). Fourth, corresponding with the sweat of his face in which the first man was to eat his bread, we learn concerning the second man, "And his sweat was as it were great drops of blood falling down to the ground" (Luke 22. 44). Fifth, just as the first Adam was to return to the dust, so the cry of the last Adam, in that wonderful prophetic Psalm, was "Thou hast brought Me into the dust of death" (Psalm 22. 15). Sixth, the sword of justice which barred the way to the tree of life was sheathed in the side of God's Son, for of old, Jehovah had said, "Awake, O sword, against My Shepherd, and against the man that is My Fellow" (Zechariah 13. 7). Seventh, the counterpart of God's original warning to Adam, namely, spiritual death, which is the separation of the soul from God, is witnessed in that most solemn of all cries, "My God, My God, Why hast Thou forsaken Me?" (Matthew 27. 46). How absolutely did our blessed Saviour identify Himself with those which were lost, took their place and suffered the Just for the unjust! How apparent it is, that Christ in His own body, did bear the curse entailed by the Fall.